# FRIENDS FOR LIFE

*Strangers Brought Together*
*by the War in Iraq*

# FRIENDS FOR LIFE

*Strangers Brought Together*
*by the War in Iraq*

Jennifer MackInday and Patti Donahue

Sandy Island Press

Bloomington, Indiana
Amado, Arizona

Book cover design by Sarah Branscum
www.sarahbranscum.com

Applicable BISAC Codes:

HIS027170     HISTORY / Military / Iraq War (2003-)

BIO008000     BIOGRAPHY & AUTOBIOGRAPHY / Military

Library of Congress Control Number 2009904125

ISBN 978-0-9824483-0-4

**PRINTED IN THE UNITED STATES OF AMERICA**

10 9 8 7 6 5 4 3 2 1

First Edition

For the soldiers and families of Deuce Four

# CONTENTS

# AUTHORS' NOTE

This is a work of non-fiction. The stories in this book are true. We have retold the events just as we have remembered them, or as they were related to us by those present at the time. Additionally, this book includes emails, instant messages, and hand-written correspondence. Portions of this book authored by Patti Donahue are italicized. Jennifer MackInday's portions of the book are in regular font.

Those interested will find resources for soldiers, veterans, and their families in our Appendix. Information and resource links may also be found on our website, www.friendsforlifebook.weebly.com.

It is our hope that sharing these memories will provide insight to the struggles faced by soldiers and their families during deployment and when they return home.

# INTRODUCTION

By Jennifer MackInday

There are many family stories emerging since the invasion of Iraq on March 20, 2003. As I sit in airports waiting for flights, I am often in the company of soldiers. Some are coming home for much needed reprieve from the war. Others are making their way back to war. Some are somber, some are strong, others anxious. All are precious.

One soldier in particular caught my eye on a cloudy June morning in St. Louis. In fact, it was D-Day, June 6th. The soldier was a Private in the Infantry, short and slim he looked more like a kid who sat next to me in math class than a soldier returning to war. He was fidgety and nervous. The way you are when you wait in the hospital while a loved one is in surgery. He was unsettled. As I stood behind him in the security line, I watched him empty his pockets of coins, money, and papers. There were many papers. I imagined they were well wishes from family, email addresses and phone numbers of pretty girls he met while home on leave. I asked him if he was coming home or going back.

"Going back Ma'am," he responded. His eyes darted uneasily as he watched guardedly for snipers, terrorists, anything dangerous.

"Thanks for your service," I chirped. "Stay safe."

"Yes ma'am," he said with a slight smile. The young soldier then headed off to the smoking room to wait for his plane. He joined several others, one man wearing a Vietnam Veteran hat. The veteran saw the soldier fumble for his cigarette and lighter, then stepped forward to offer one of his own. A small comforting gesture that I hoped would ease the young man's tension. After he finished his smoke, the soldier shook hands with the veteran and strolled out of the smoking room, down the corridor and out of sight.

I prayed for him silently as I waited in the terminal for my flight. I prayed he would return to his family, friends, and perhaps the pretty girl whose phone number was written on one of the crumpled notes in the soldier's pocket. In my heart, I knew he may not return. If he did return, I knew he would forever be changed.

In the summer of 1998, my fourteen-year old brother moved in with me. Our parents had just divorced and my little brother needed a home. The move to my house was easy, at first. It became more difficult as my role of a parent increased and my role as a sister started to fade. His grades were bad and although he played for the high school football team, he did not have a direction for his life. College was certainly not in his future, and with few life skills, there was little hope for anything more than a minimum wage job.

"You've hardly got any options," I yelled one evening in response to a poor report card. "Your only choice is to go in the military." Well, that is exactly what he did. Just after 9-11, my little brother joined the US Army. He left high school early and headed for basic training at Ft. Benning in March 2002. By March of the next year, he was a fully trained soldier, and our country was at war.

When my brother deployed to Iraq in October of 2004, his life turned upside down, and so did mine. Even though we were thousands of miles apart, we embarked on a journey together. Along the way, his brigade survived many hardships and fought as hard as any before and since.

During the yearlong deployment of 1$^{st}$ Battalion, 24$^{th}$ Infantry Regiment, 1$^{st}$ Brigade, 25$^{th}$ Infantry Division Stryker Brigade Combat Team, or Deuce Four, the soldiers played a crucial role in the battle for Mosul, a

Sunni dominated city of approximately 2 million people. According to Battalion Commander Lieutenant Colonel Michael Erik Kurilla, the soldiers faced 3,056 enemy attacks, discovered 1,335 improvised explosive devices and 84 suicide vehicle-borne explosive devices, endured 1,513 direct-fire attacks and 631 indirect fire attacks. The brigade detained 3,050 enemies, including 179 high-level terrorist leaders and al-Qaeda commander Abu Talha. They rescued nine kidnapping victims, and killed 550 enemies in action - more than any other brigade in this war.

Deuce Four also spent time in the communities surrounding Mosul, providing medical services to over 2,000 Iraqi children. The brigade built 415 building projects totaling over $72 million, including schools, bridges, roads and hospitals.

Fifty-six brave soldiers died in battle for Mosul. Of approximately 700 soldiers deployed with Deuce Four, 181 were killed or wounded. The brigade received many medals and awards including 181 Purple Hearts and the Valorous Unit Award. During the battle for Mosul, Deuce Four faced some of the heaviest fighting of the war in Iraq.

# DEDICATION TO THE FALLEN

## by Patti Donahue

*There seems to be a common trend among heroes of war. No matter which war, and no matter how courageous a soldier's own amazing actions, it is always a fallen comrade that soldiers point to as the REAL hero. Left behind are wives, fiancés, mothers, fathers, children, siblings, and extended families with a Family HERO who will be forever frozen in time. Each hero's death ceaselessly affecting the lives of the many people with whom they were connected. It is to the loved ones of these soldiers, who wake up every morning with their loss, who find ways to continue living and contributing, and who lay their heads down each night with thoughts of their lost soldier to whom we dedicate this book. THEY are OUR heroes.*

*The lives of these fifty-six soldiers were sacrificed in or near Mosul, Iraq, from November 2004 through August 2005.*

**Steven E. Auchman**, 37, Waterloo, New York, Master Sergeant, US Air Force, 5th Air Support Operations Squadron, died November 9, 2004, from injuries received when multiple rocket propelled grenades struck his location in Mosul, Iraq.

**Horst G. "Gary" Moore**, 38, San Antonio, Texas, Major, US Army, 1st Battalion, 24th Infantry Regiment, 1st Brigade, 25th Infantry Division SBCT, died November 9, 2004, from injuries received when an enemy mortar attack struck his unit's living area in Mosul, Iraq.

**Thomas K. Doerflinger**, 20, Silver Spring, Maryland, Specialist, US Army, 1st Battalion, 24th Infantry Regiment, 1st Brigade, 25th Infantry Division SBCT, died November 11, 2004, when his unit received small arms fire while conducting combat operations in Mosul, Iraq.

**Jose Ricardo Flores-Mejia**, 21, Santa Clarita, California, Private First Class, US Army, 25th Transportation Company, died November 16, 2004, when a makeshift bomb hit his convoy in Mosul, Iraq.

**George D. Harrison**, 22, Knoxville, Tennessee, Private First Class, US Army, 293rd Military Police Company, 3rd Military Police Battalion (Provisional), 3rd Infantry Division, died December 2, 2004, when his Humvee was attacked by enemy forces using small arms fire in Mosul, Iraq.

**David A. Mitts**, 24, Hammond, Oregon, Sergeant, US Army, 3rd Battalion, 21st Infantry Regiment, 1st Brigade, 25th Infantry Division, died December 4, 2004, when his Stryker received enemy fire during convoy operations in Mosul, Iraq.

**Salamo J. Tuialuuluu**,23, Pago Pago, American Samoa, Staff Sergeant, US Army, 3rd Battalion, 21st Infantry Regiment, 1st Brigade, 25th Infantry Division, died December 4, 2004, when his Stryker received enemy fire during convoy operations in Mosul, Iraq.

**Patrick D. Leach**, 39, Rock Hill, South Carolina, Chief Warrant Officer, South Carolina National Guard, 1st Battalion, 151st Aviation Regiment, died December 9, 2004, after being involved in an Apache helicopter accident in Mosul, Iraq.

**Andrew C. Shields**, 25, Campobello, South Carolina, First Lieutenant, South Carolina National Guard, 1st Battalion, 151st Aviation Regiment, died December 9, 2004, after being involved in an Apache helicopter accident in Mosul, Iraq.

**Lionel Ayro**, 22, Jeanerette, Louisiana, Private First Class, US Army, 73rd Engineer Company, 1st Brigade, 25th Infantry Division, died December 21, 2004, when a suicide bomber attacked the dining hall at FOB Marez, Mosul, Iraq.

**Joel E. Baldwin**, 37, Arlington, Virginia, Chief Petty Officer, US Navy, Mobile Construction Battalion 7, died December 21, 2004, when a suicide bomber attacked the dining hall at FOB Marez, Mosul, Iraq.

**Jonathan Castro**, 21, Corona, California, Specialist, US Army, 73rd Engineer Company, 1st Brigade, 25th Infantry Division, died December 21, 2004, when a suicide bomber attacked the dining hall at FOB Marez, Mosul, Iraq.

**Thomas J. Dostie**, 20, Sommerville, Maine, Specialist, Maine National Guard, 133rd Engineer Battalion, died December 21, 2004, when a suicide bomber attacked the dining hall at FOB Marez, Mosul, Iraq.

**Cory M. Hewitt**, 26, Stewart, Tennessee, Specialist, US Army, 705th Ordnance Company, US Army, died Tuesday, December 21, 2004, when a suicide bomber attacked the dining hall at FOB Marez, Mosul, Iraq.

**William W. Jacobsen Jr.**, 31, Charlotte, North Carolina, Captain,1st Battalion, 24th Infantry Regiment, 1st Brigade, 25th Infantry Division SBCT, died December 21, 2004, when a suicide bomber attacked the dining hall at FOB Marez, Mosul, Iraq.

7

**Robert S. Johnson**, 23, Seaside, California, Staff Sergeant, US Army,1st Battalion, 24th Infantry Regiment, 1st Brigade, 25th Infantry Division SBCT, died December 21, 2004, when a suicide bomber attacked the dining hall at FOB Marez, Mosul, Iraq.

**Paul D. Karpowich**, 30, Bridgeport, Pennsylvania, Sergeant First Class, US Army Reserves, 2nd Battalion, 390th Infantry Regiment, died December 21, 2004, when a suicide bomber attacked the dining hall at FOB Marez, Mosul, Iraq.

**Nicholas C. Mason**, 20, King George, Virginia, Specialist, Virginia National Guard, 276th Engineer Battalion, died December 21, 2004, when a suicide bomber attacked the dining hall at FOB Marez, Mosul, Iraq.

**Julian S. Melo**, 47, Brooklyn, New York, Staff Sergeant, US Army,1st Battalion, 5th Infantry Regiment, 1st Brigade, 25th Infantry Division, died December 21, 2004, when a suicide bomber attacked the dining hall at FOB Marez, Mosul, Iraq.

**Robert D. O'Dell,** 38, Manassas, Virginia, Sergeant Major, US Army Intelligence and Security Command, died December 21, 2004, when a suicide bomber attacked the dining hall at FOB Marez, Mosul, Iraq.

**Lynn R. Poulin Sr.,** 47, Freedom, Maine, Sergeant, Maine National Guard, 133rd Engineer Battalion, died December 21, 2004, when a suicide bomber attacked the dining hall at FOB Marez, Mosul, Iraq.

**David A. Ruhren,** 20, Stafford, Virginia, Specialist, Virginia National Guard, 276th Engineer Battalion, died December 21, 2004, when a suicide bomber attacked the dining hall at FOB Marez, Mosul, Iraq.

**Darren D. VanKomen**, 33, Bluefield, West Virginia, Staff Sergeant, US Army, 2$^{nd}$ Squadron, 14$^{th}$ Cavalry Regiment, 1$^{st}$ Brigade, 25$^{th}$ Infantry Division, died December 21, 2004, when a suicide bomber attacked the dining hall at FOB Marez, Mosul, Iraq.

**Oscar Sanchez**, 19, Modesto, California, Private First Class, US Army, 1$^{st}$ Battalion, 24$^{th}$ Infantry Regiment, 1$^{st}$ Brigade, 25$^{th}$ Infantry Division SBCT, died December 29, 2004, when a vehicle-borne IED struck his observation post in Mosul, Iraq.

**Cory R. Depew**, 21, Beech Grove, Indiana, Private, US Army, 2$^{nd}$ Squadron, 14$^{th}$ Cavalry Regiment, 1$^{st}$ Brigade, 25$^{th}$ Infantry Division, died January 4, 2005, when his Stryker was struck by a RPG in Tal Afar, near Mosul, Iraq.

**Gunnar D. Becker**, 19, Forestburg, South Dakota, Private First Class, US Army, 2$^{nd}$ Battalion, 63$^{rd}$ Armor Regiment, 1$^{st}$ Infantry Division, died January 13, 2005, of non-combat related injuries in Mosul, Iraq.

**Brian A. Mack**, 36, Phoenix, Arizona, Sergeant First Class, US Army, 3$^{rd}$ Battalion, 21$^{st}$ Infantry Regiment, 1$^{st}$ Brigade, 25$^{th}$ Infantry Division, died January 13, 2005, when his military vehicle was hit by an IED in Mosul, Iraq.

**Nathaniel T. Swindell**, 24, Bronx, New York, Sergeant, US Army, 1$^{st}$ Battalion, 24$^{th}$ Infantry Regiment, 1$^{st}$ Brigade, 25$^{th}$ Infantry Division SBCT, died January 15, 2005, from a non-hostile injury in Mosul, Iraq.

**Nainoa K. Hoe**, 27, Kailua, Hawaii, First Lieutenant, US Army, 3$^{rd}$ Battalion, 21$^{st}$ Infantry Regiment, 1$^{st}$ Brigade, 25$^{th}$ Infantry Division, died January 22, 2005, of wounds received when he was attacked by enemy forces using small arms fire in Mosul, Iraq.

**Mickey E. Zaun**, 27, Brooklyn Park, Minnesota, Sergeant First Class, US Army Special Operations Command, died January 28, 2005, from injuries sustained in a collision between two armored vehicles in Mosul, Iraq.

**Stephen R. Sherman**, 27, Neptune, New Jersey, Sergeant, US Army, 1st Battalion, 5th Infantry Regiment, 1st Brigade, 25th Infantry Division, died February 3, 2005, from wounds sustained when an IED detonated near his vehicle in Mosul, Iraq.

**Zachary R. Wobler**, 24, Ottawa, Ohio, Staff Sergeant, US Army, 2nd Battalion, 325th Airborne Infantry Regiment, 82nd Airborne Division, died February 6, 2005, when his dismounted patrol encountered enemy forces using small arms fire in Mosul, Iraq.

**Adam J. Plumondore**, 22, Gresham, Oregon, Sergeant, US Army, 1st Battalion, 24th Infantry Regiment, 1st Brigade, 25th Infantry Division SBCT, died February 16, 2005, when a vehicle-borne IED detonated near his vehicle in Mosul, Iraq.

**Frank B. Hernandez**, 21, Phoenix, Arizona, Sergeant, US Army, 2nd Squadron, 14th Cavalry Regiment, 1st Brigade, 25th Infantry Division17, 2005, died February 17, 2005, when an IED detonated near his vehicle in Tal Afar, near Mosul, Iraq.

**Clint R. Gertson**, 26, Houston, Texas, Specialist, US Army, 1st Battalion, 24th Infantry Regiment, 1st Brigade, 25th Infantry Division SBCT, died February 19, 2005, from injuries sustained from enemy forces small arms fire in Mosul, Iraq.

**Juan M. Solorio**, 32, Dallas Texas, Staff Sergeant, US Army, 3rd Battalion, 21st Infantry Regiment, 1st Brigade, 25th Infantry

Division, died March 4, 2005, when an IED detonated near his military vehicle as his unit was being attacked by enemy forces using small arms fire in Mosul, Iraq.

**Donald D. Griffith Jr.**, 29, Mechanicsville, Iowa, Staff Sergeant, US Army, 2nd Squadron, 14th Cavalry Regiment, 1st Brigade, 25th Infantry Division, died March 11, 2005, as a result of hostile action in Tal Afar, near Mosul, Iraq.

**Rocky D. Payne**, 26, Howell, Utah, Specialist, US Army, 497th Transportation Company, 44th Corps Support Battalion, 1st COSCOM, died March 16, 2005, at a military hospital in Baghdad, Iraq, from injuries sustained when an IED detonated by his Humvee in Mosul, Iraq.

**Kenneth L. Ridgley**, 30, Olney, Illinois, Sergeant, US Army, 3rd Battalion, 21st Infantry Regiment, 1st Brigade, 25th Infantry Division, died March 30, 2005 of injuries sustained when enemy forces using small arms fire attacked his unit in Mosul, Iraq.

**Ioasa F. Tavae Jr.**, 29, Pago Pago, American Samoa, Staff Sergeant, US Army, 1st Battalion, 5th Infantry Regiment, 1st Brigade, 25th Infantry Division, died April 2, 2005, when his unit was attacked by enemy forces using small arms fire in Tal Afar, near Mosul, Iraq.

**Gavin J. Colburn**, 20, Waverly, Ohio, Private First Class, US Army Reserves, 542nd Transportation Company, died April 22, 2005, along a supply route when an IED device detonated near his convoy vehicle in Mosul, Iraq.

**Anthony J. Davis Jr.**, 22, Long Beach, California, Sergeant, US Army, 1st Battalion, 24th Infantry Regiment, 1st Brigade, 25th Infantry Division SBCT, died April 23, 2005 when a vehicle-borne IED detonated near his Stryker in Mosul, Iraq.

**William A. Edens**, 29, Columbia, Missouri, First Lieutenant, US Army, 1st Battalion, 5th Infantry Regiment, 1st Brigade, 25th Infantry Division, died April 28, 2005, when an IED detonated near his Stryker in Tal Afar, near Mosul, Iraq.

**Eric W. Morris**, 31, Sparks, Nevada, Sergeant, US Army, 1st Battalion, 5th Infantry Regiment, 1st Brigade, 25th Infantry Division, died April 28, 2005, when an IED detonated near his Stryker in Tal Afar, near Mosul, Iraq.

**Robert W. Murray Jr.**, 21, Westfield, Indiana, Private First Class, US Army 2nd Squadron, 3rd Armor Cavalry Regiment, died April 28, 2005, when an IED detonated near his Stryker in Tal Afar, near Mosul, Iraq.

**Ricky W. Rockholt Jr.**, 28, Winston, Oregon, Specialist, US Army, 2nd Squadron, 3rd Armor Cavalry Regiment, died April 28, 2005, when an IED detonated near his Stryker in Tal Afar, near Mosul, Iraq.

**Michael J. Bordelon**, 37, Morgan City, Louisiana, First Sergeant, US Army, 1st Battalion, 24th Infantry Regiment, 1st Brigade, 25th Infantry Division SBCT, died May 10, 2005, at Brooke Army Medical Center, San Antonio, Texas, from injuries sustained April 23, 2005, when a vehicle-borne IED detonated near his Stryker in Mosul, Iraq.

**Tyler L. Creamean**, 21, Jacksonville, Arkansas, Specialist, US Army, 73rd Engineer Company, 1st Brigade, 25th Infantry Division, died May 22, 2005, from injuries sustained when an IED detonated near his Humvee in Mosul, Iraq.

**Benjamin C. Morton**, 24, Wright, Kansas, Sergeant, US Army, 1st Battalion, 24th Infantry Regiment, 1st Brigade, 25th Infantry

12

Division SBCT, died May 22, 2005, when his dismounted patrol encountered enemy small arms fire in Mosul, Iraq.

**Aaron N. Seesan,** 25, Massillon, Ohio, First Lieutenant, US Army, 73$^{rd}$ Engineer Company, 1$^{st}$ Brigade, 25$^{th}$ Infantry Division, died May 22, 2005, at Landstuhl Medical Center from injuries sustained when an IED detonated near his Humvee in Mosul, Iraq.

**Phillip Sayles,** 26, Jacksonville, Arkansas, Specialist, US Army, 1$^{st}$ Battalion, 24$^{th}$ Infantry Regiment, 1$^{st}$ Brigade, 25$^{th}$ Infantry Division SBCT, died May 28, 2005, when an IED detonated near his security position in Mosul, Iraq.

**Nils G. Thompson,** 19, Confluence, Pennsylvania, Private First Class, US Army, 1$^{st}$ Battalion, 24$^{th}$ Infantry Regiment, 1$^{st}$ Brigade, 25$^{th}$ Infantry Division SBCT, died August 4, 2005, when he was struck by enemy sniper fire while on a routine patrol at an Iraqi police station in Mosul, Iraq.

**Jose L. Ruiz,** 28, Brentwood, New York, Specialist, US Army, 3$^{rd}$ Battalion, 21$^{st}$ Infantry Regiment, 1$^{st}$ Brigade, 25$^{th}$ Infantry Division, died August 15, 2005, when he was conducting security operations and enemy forces using small arms fire drove by his position in a civilian vehicle in Mosul, Iraq.

**Elden D. Arcand,** 22, White Bear Lake, Minnesota, Private First Class, US Army, 306$^{th}$ Transportation Company, 68$^{th}$ Corps Support Battalion, 43$^{rd}$ Area Support Group, died August 21, 2005, when the tractor/tanker in which he was riding rolled over in Mosul, Iraq.

**Brian L. Morris,** 38, Centreville, Michigan, Staff Sergeant, US Army, 306$^{th}$ Transportation Company, 68$^{th}$ Corps Support Battalion, 43$^{rd}$ Area Support Group, died August 21, 2005, when the tractor/tanker in which he was riding rolled over in Mosul, Iraq.

**Jason E. Ames**, 21, Cerulean, Kentucky, Specialist, US Army, 3rd Battalion, 21st Infantry Regiment, 1st Brigade, 25th Infantry Division, died on Aug. 31, 2005, from non-combat related injuries in Mosul, Iraq.

# DEPLOYMENT

Driving in a hard pouring rain on winding rural
roads in Southern Indiana while traveling for work, I
tried my hardest to keep the upcoming deployment of
my brother's Army brigade out of my mind.
Although I did not know the exact deployment date –
no one did – I knew it would be any day. Nearly three
years earlier, my brother, James, enlisted in the US
Army. Up until that point, our family was blessed
with the rare post-911 opportunity of having a family
member in the service that had not yet been deployed
to the Middle East. That ended with the phone call
my brother made that chilly, wet afternoon. As I was
driving through nowhere it seemed my brother was
headed into the unknown.

My cell phone rang and my heart sank. It was the call
I had been dreading for months. Deuce Four was
leaving for Iraq. My brother, James, and a few fellow
soldiers were having a 'last meal' of sorts with some
girlfriends at a Ft. Lewis area fast food restaurant.
Soaking up Americana and phoning home to say
goodbye was all they had left to do before boarding
the buses that would transport the brigade to the
airfield. The next stop would be Iraq.

15

My fears for James during the deployment to Iraq were numerous. Obviously, I worried that he would be killed or severely wounded. In fact, there were many times when I was convinced that he would never come home. I also worried about James mental health. Having a sound mind keeps you alert – staying alert keeps you alive. Having decided that communications from home would be the key to keeping James as focused as possible, I wondered in what way we would be able to communicate. James learned from friends previously deployed that phone calls would be rare. The family readiness group from Ft. Lewis told us that mail was important, but could take weeks to arrive. How could I communicate effectively with my brother if we hardly spoke and my letters and packages took weeks to arrive? The answer came in the form of an email.

**Dear Jenn,**

**You know my Yahoo email address, so I want you to sign up for Yahoo Instant Message. Practically everyone here has IM and I only have to wait in line an hour or two to get on the computer. The line for the phones is like four hours long, so sign-up for instant message and we can talk online, okay? -James**

With the hope of communication more frequent than the occasional email or phone call, I quickly acquainted myself with instant messaging. This was my way of staying as close to James as possible despite the separation of time, location, and circumstance.

The day Deuce Four deployed to Iraq was dreary in Indiana, where I lived, thousands of miles away from Ft. Lewis. Southern Indiana is usually so pretty in October that the cold rain was a slap in my face. It is even gloomier this day because my brother is now a soldier deployed to Iraq. I spend the day working hard in the hopes that my mind will be free of worry. Of course that does not work. However, in the evening when I return home I hear my computer sounding an alert. My newly installed instant messaging program has received a message! Hooray! The message is from Iraq. My brother is safe and we soon have our first online conversation.

**IM – Jenn and James, October 2004**

**Jenn: Oh good - you are online. I have to travel for work today and I was afraid I would miss you. Maybe you will get your 1st package soon- I sent it 3 weeks ago**

**James: Maybe...I sure hope so**

Jenn: What is the weather like today?

James: hot - 104 degrees here

Jenn: Wow! That is hot! I gave your friends from school your address

James: Good...I hope they write. We are going to be moving soon.

Jenn: Will you address change when you move?

James: The APO number I gave you will stay the same but the FOB name will be different, I can't tell you now for security so I'll tell you later

Jenn: What is FOB?

James: Forward Operating Base

Jenn: Okay, well I think your mail will get to you as long as the APO is right - I will just use the unit number and the APO

James: That's pretty much all you need to get mail to me anyway.

Jenn: Did you sleep well last night? Your 1st care package has a pillow

James: Good, a pillow would be nice

Jenn: You sound down - are you okay?

James: Yeah...just routine here. I heard my first explosion yesterday

Jenn: I bet that was scary- there were not any casualty reports yesterday; I assume no one was hurt

James: Nah...It just shook the ground

Jenn: Does it sound like thunder?

James: Yeah, you could feel it

Jenn: Do Iraqi's go to work, school, and stuff?

James: Yeah

Jenn: I would not like to go to work or school with explosions going on

James: Can you send a small fan for my hatch? It gets hot with the hatch down

Jenn:Okay, I'll get one with a mount/Velcro

James: They are showing a movie here tonight

Jenn: Does the Army have good food there?

James: The food isn't bad - better than basic and they had shrimp on Sunday.

Jenn: Do the Iraqi National Guard eat with you?

James: Yes, they do

**Jenn: Do they speak English? Do you think you will learn any Iraqi?**

**James: Yeah, some do, and I don't know...probably**

**Jenn: Are there any foreigner soldiers with you?**

**James: Yes, some from Australia and Turkey**

**Jenn: It must be weird all those different people all together**

**James: Yeah, it is weird. Hey, I have to go now**

**Jenn: Love you, bye for now**

**James: OK have a good day**

With that, my first conversation ended. I learned a lot in that first chat. Most importantly, I learned that some things James would not be able to say to me and that when he had to go it would feel like my heart had been ripped out. I decided to save each of our online conversations as text files because I did not know when or if I would chat with him again.

Letters to friends and family back home have always been the most informative look into life behind the lines. In this war, it was not handwritten letters keeping us informed, but emails and instant messages. Fortunately, my brother was able to logon

20

frequently. In fact, we were able to chat the very next day.

IM – Jenn and James, October 2004

Jenn: Hi there

James: Hey Jenn! We are having bad weather right now - a sand storm

Jenn: Yuck! Do you have goggles?

James:No, I only have my sunglasses and a bandanna that dad sent me before I left

Jenn: I will send you some goggles - I saw some on the family support site

James: Oh good because sand sucks. We stayed inside our buildings today cause of the storm.

Jenn: Do you guys have a web cam?

James: Nope – we are lucky they have internet access here

Jenn: If you get access to a web cam let me know and I will buy one here

James: OK...they may have them at the other FOB we are moving to

Jenn: Yeah that is what I think. I looked up the city in Iraq where your friend's mom said your battalion is moving to and it does not look good. There are several FOBs in the area, but the city sucks. Very dangerous.

James: How did she know what city we are going to move to?

Jenn: I am not sure how she knew, I did not really think to ask

James: I do not know how you know where we are going, security is supposed to be tight here – I guess it is not, huh?

Jenn: I read things in the chat rooms from the wives/moms of other soldiers

James: Oh, OK

Jenn: They do say stuff sometimes and I think they should not put that information on the internet - the terrorists probably are on there too - sometimes the webmaster takes stuff off, but a lot of stuff gets through

James: Are there chat rooms just for certain brigades to use?

Jenn: Yeah, you can get on a bulletin board with families of A-Company... there are several pages for 1/24 and I've met several relatives of soldiers in A-Company

James: Like who?

Jenn: Well, Jon's folks, and some other people. On the front page of that website, they post news from around the world that includes stuff on Strykers, that helps me stay informed...there are also good ideas from 3$^{rd}$ brigade's families on what to send in care packages. You know pal, I just can't stand the news right now. There is so much crap about the Presidential election.

James: Yeah and about Iraq

Jenn: It is rough there, isn't it?

James: Yeah...but I'm fine

Jenn: I know there is no need to worry - I know you are okay

James: I'm tough.

Jenn: You are well trained.

James: We are well trained. I've been training almost 3 years.

Jenn: I know. That is amazing isn't it? It seems like just yesterday I was lecturing you in the kitchen about the Army and the ASVAB tests.

James: Well now look at me-I'm in a frickin' desert!

Jenn: I'm so sorry about that.

James: I'm good...only 364 days left!

Jenn: I am glad to see that you still have a sense
of humor. So far, you are doing a great job of
staying in touch with me. I couldn't be happier
except if you weren't in Iraq, of course!

James: Good. Well I have to go...love ya...

Jenn: Take care - love you!

When our boys first deployed we didn't know many
details of their upcoming assignment. There were a
lot of rumors on the internet, some of them true
others way off base. It was difficult to know exactly
what was happening unless we heard it directly from
our soldiers. It didn't take long to learn that our boys
would be on very dangerous missions every day, for
the entire deployment.

We asked Jon why the attacks in Mosul were so
frequent when they arrived. What did the previous
brigade do compared to what Deuce Four did?

*"The previous unit was a cavalry unit. Their
attitude is 'Roll or Die', which means you never
stop the vehicle. You just keep driving and push
through anything. This turns things into a kind of
game, like at the fair. The calvary vehicles are just*

*the ducks going by in a row. The terrorists just take their time and shoot at them. The difference is that what we had to do was get out of the vehicle and then kick in doors like a SWAT team coming in, and then search the entire home. It was a big change for the terrorists, because we would actually get out of our vehicles, and we could find their hidden caches of weapons and destroy them. Because we were destroying a lot of the weapons that they were using against us, of course, the attacks went down because they didn't have as much ammo to attack us."*

I asked my brother James about the nature of their missions and how it felt to be inside an Iraqi home conducting raids.

**"A lot of times you know they were real good about letting us come in. Sometimes it was in the middle of the night and we would have to wake everyone up, which is bad because everyone is grumpy when they wake up, you know. There were a lot of weapons and ammo and stuff that we found on those raids, and because they would try to hide it we had to look everywhere. It's no fun to turn over someone's refrigerator right in front of them and just basically destroy all their food and wreck up their whole house and**

everything, but we had to do it. I would be really pissed if someone came into our house and just tore everything up like that. Anyway, sometimes people were nice and we didn't find anything and then we just moved on. Once we were on the roof of this house and a kid that lived there came up and had some drinks for us...that was real nice, you know."

I can't imagine the intensity and stress of these raids. To experience not only your own terror, but to witness it daily in the eyes of others must be something that will always haunt our soldiers. I thought often during the deployment of how Iraqi civilians were affected by our military actions. I felt guilt about how these poor, innocent people were being treated. I felt selfish because I knew our boys needed to find hidden weapons caches so they could be safer during deployment.

Those constant feelings of intermingling emotions were difficult for me to handle. Luckily, I met several other family members early in the deployment. Although we were perfect strangers, the soldiers we loved were serving together and those ties bound us tighter than we could ever have imagined. In the first few weeks, we learned how to keep vigil online, and to communicate with each other whenever possible.

*My cell phone rang and I knew it was my middle son
calling to say goodbye.*

**"Hi Mom," Jon said. "Just calling to say goodbye,
we ship out tomorrow. I'm not sure when we can
talk again. I will try to call you from Germany on
the way to Kuwait, but who knows? By the way, I
had to leave my car with Janet, a friend, and I
don't know how long she can keep it. I hope you
can find a way to take care of it."**

*Inside I was thinking, "Not now. You cannot cry now.
Wait until this call is over. He needs you to be strong."*

*To my son I said, "OK son, we will figure out something,
don't worry, we love you and we are so proud of you.
Travel safely. Call us when you can. Will anyone be there
to see you off at the buses? We are so sorry we cannot be
there." Regrettably, a trip from our home in Arizona to the
send-off wasn't possible. Our family would say good-bye as
thousands of other families were forced to, over the phone.*

*"Some girls James and I met will be at the send-off. Becki
and Ashley will be there to see us off, don't worry."*

*As strongly as I could I said, "OK son, I am glad for that.
Thanks for the call. We will be praying for you, son. Keep
your head down and be safe."*

27

*Jon whispered, "I love you and dad so much. I didn't realize how much until now. Bye, Mom."*

*The much anticipated, dreaded phone call was over.*

*Oh dear God, what do we do now, I thought. And so, the year long Odyssey of worry, tears, panic, held breaths, constant praying, and waking up instantly to the sound of a Yahoo Instant Messenger knock began.*

*It was October 20, 2004, and Deuce Four was on the way to Iraq. At the time, it was thought they would be stationed in the north of Iraq, near the Syrian border. Almost 5,000 American soldiers were on their way to a country that felt invaded, to try to do their job. The battles at Fallujah were all in the news as the Marines were surrounding the city to take control. Little did we know the offensive south of the location to which our troops were headed, would mean significant changes in the mission of our soldiers.*

*While the Marines prepared for their offensive, Deuce Four continued their travels to begin their deployment. Many enemy forces escaped Fallujah and went North, in hordes, taking over every single police station in Mosul. As soon as our units arrived in country, they were quickly redirected to Mosul to try to regain some control of the city. Initially it was complete chaos.*

*Meantime, at home, the families had an address that was wrong, had heard little to nothing from their soldiers, and began adapting to a totally new routine of life. Constant fear and dread ruled the hearts of the moms, sisters, fathers, brothers, grandparents, aunts, uncles, cousins and friends of each of these nearly 5,000 soldiers. This was an awesome and largely ignored personal impact on each of these relatives that was unknown to the majority of the country. An enormous and urgent need for information, council, and consolation grew like a deep fissure. From this great need, survival alliances began to develop. Surprisingly, our first contact with Jon did not come by phone, but rather through Instant Messenger.*

*I was at work, and my husband Tom, called to say, "Jon is online, thank God, he is OK. I am chatting with him now. I will save the conversation. See you tonight, honey. I've got to go."*

*"OH GOD, keep Jon safe and give me strength to go on," I quickly prayed. I felt relief, jealousy, worry, hurt, happiness, and an ocean of emotions swirled in my head. Then stop it, stop it, stop it, I thought. I had to focus and finish my work. Another quick prayer for control and with a deep cleansing breath I focused on finishing my day at work.*

*Finally, the day ended and I drove home feeling the same excitement I used to feel when heading home to take over for Tom or a baby sitter back when my boys were babies. Way back then, I would be so excited to catch up on the progress for the day; like seeing the baby sit up, roll over and the like. But now, the "baby" was a man, whose job was that of a soldier. And the progress was reading a copy of the instant message between my husband Tom and my son Jon. Then Tom and I would discuss and try to extract from the few words, how our son was faring. Mostly we were discouraged, distressed, and overcome with a helpless feeling, but these IMs were islands of comfort in a huge ocean of despair and we lived for the next contact.*

*After re-reading the message, and allowing a second brief time of relief to pass, we would talk about how wonderful technology was to allow an instant messenger chat with our son, half a world away. As we discussed the conditions Jon was enduring, and the news of the day, we began to recognize a way to help fill the void of constant worry and wonder about our son. From then on, each time Jon chatted with us, we would ask, "Who is your battle buddy today?" We would ask if we could add the "battle buddy" soldier to our Yahoo friends list. We also asked who our son Jon was chatting with and would they let us add them to our IM list, too?" Little by little, person by person, a new network of Army friends and family began to grow. These friends became our lifeline and means of keeping tabs, as much as possible, on our soldiers, so far away and in such constant peril.*

*One of the people we met through this process was Ashley, a young woman who lived near Ft. Lewis in Tacoma, Washington. Ashley and another young lady named Becki spent time prior to the deployment with Jon and his platoon-mate, James. James was from Indiana, and had been raised by his older sister Jennifer. We would later meet Jennifer, or Jenn, and a strong friendship would grow. But, at this time, right at deployment, we were just loved ones of soldiers. We were unaware of each other's parallel struggles.*

*Just before deployment, Jon and James took friends Ashley and Becki on a trip in Jon's car to Oregon. Several bad decisions, such as being outside the allowed perimeter from Ft. Lewis, and driving a small, overloaded car, too long and too fast, resulted in a serious car breakdown several hundred miles from base. Jon called us, but we were too far away to help. Finally, he and James got in touch with a soldier named Clint from Texas, who drove all the way there and towed Jon's car back to Ft. Lewis. He only accepted a few bucks for gas money, essentially helping his brother soldier out of the kindness of his heart. Jon's 1996 Honda Civic with two rods poking out of the engine was one of several interesting puzzles left by our deployed son*

31

*that we had to solve from our home in Arizona, a distance of 1,800 miles from Ft Lewis.*

*In the first months of deployment, we were so consumed by worry and adjustment to our new life as "Blue Star" parents that the problems with Jon's car moved to the back burner. A very nice lady named Janet, had kindly told Jon that his car could stay in her extra parking space at her apartment complex until someone complained. When the complaints came, we began to explore our options. To shorten the story, I will just say, the options were few and none too viable.*

*Tom, my husband, who was retired and stayed home during the day, would man the computer, watching for Jon or any of his comrades to get online. In the evening and on weekends, I would man the computer. Through the night, while we slept, the computer was always on with Instant Messenger activated. If we heard the KNOCK showing a contact on the friend list was active, we were up like lightning bolts checking to see if it was Jon or any of our other "adopted" sons were online.*

*Soldiers in combat do NOT have regular hours. Sometimes their missions were during the daytime, other times nighttime, and sometimes the missions lasted days in a row. So setting up a schedule was not possible. The loved ones at home simply put their own lives on hold and waited for the precious moments of contact. We learned to forward our land line home phones to our cell phones, to set up our instant messaging accounts to send messages to our phones. We wracked ourselves in guilt over the occasional time when our soldier called or left an IM message and we were NOT THERE for them. We helped each other by passing messages back and forth between our families.*

*IM – Jon and Jenn, April 13, 2005*

**Jenn: Hi Jon - your mom is teaching a class today - she wanted me to let you know**

**Jon:   Oh, I see, that would explain it (why she's not online). How are you doing?**

**Jenn: I'm doing okay - thanks - missing James a lot. I know he's in good hands. Your mom sure has been nice to me - seems like she must be a great mom!!**

**Jon: Well I would ask for another one but she will do!**

**Jenn: How are you doing?**

**Jon:   I am good**

**Jenn: Good! I just called your mom and she said she's sorry she won't be able to chat with you today, but she loves you - take care of yourself.**

*Jon: Well I am going to go down and try to use the phones if the line isn't too long. If you get a chance, tell my parents I love them and will try to talk to them soon*

*Jenn: Okay, nice chatting - take care Jon*

While we waited, we watched for relatives of other soldiers to login. Often, we would chat to pass the time. We gathered information and ideas, and generally supported each other. Tom "met" Jon's friend Ashley online and started chatting with her. Soon, we both were chatting with Ashley regularly on IM. Of course, since she was in the Ft Lewis area, we asked if she could help find someone honest to fix Jon's car. Ashley was a very sweet and charming young lady, with great follow through.

If Ashley says she will do something, you could count on it. This was in sharp contrast with other friends that Jon had. One day, when Tom was lucky enough to be chatting with Jon online, he told Jon that Ashley was a doll, and how she and her family were helping with the car. Tom asked Jon why he had not dated Ashley while in Ft. Lewis. Jon responded that he thought he had probably chosen the wrong girl.

My husband Tom likes to think of himself as the strong and sober one, who would never meddle in his sons' love lives, but let me tell you, except for not having the wings, bow

34

*and arrow, Tom was a regular Cupid. He covertly worked
to help bring Jon and Ashley together. He even told Ashley
that Jon thought he had picked the wrong girl. After a long
pause, Ashley responded, "Excuse me for the delay, but I
had to pick myself up off the floor." She was thrilled.*

*The next thing we knew, Jon and Ashley "found" each
other online and were chatting often. Today, it makes me
laugh aloud every time Tom sternly tells me, "Don't
meddle in their lives Patti," if he thinks I am trying to act
like a matchmaker. HA! That rebuke will never work on me
again!*

*After several months of coordination by telephone, we
ordered an engine online for Jon's broken down car. We had
the engine shipped to the mechanic recommended by
Ashley's dad and eventually put a close to that dilemma.*

*The beautiful part of this story is the wonderful friendship
with Ashley that grew from the "pile of ashes" of the car
story like a colorful, vibrant Phoenix. While it was playing
out, the situation seemed bleak, but there was a wonderful
"dividend". Adding Ashley to our lives has been a huge
bonus.*

*The gift of true and lasting friendship emerging from the
stress and angst of deployment was a ray of hope.*

# PREPARING FOR WAR

After James was assigned to the Stryker Brigade at Fort Lewis, I got comfortable with him safely stationed in the US. You see, the Stryker vehicles were new. Strykers had never been used in combat, and they had not yet completed combat readiness training. That was comforting. After over two years into his contract, I thought James might never be deployed to Iraq or Afghanistan before his three-year contract expired. Of course, I was wrong.

Waiting for the Strykers to be deemed ready for combat was excruciating for the soldiers in Deuce Four. Many of them wanted to join their fellow soldiers in Afghanistan or Iraq. Part of the field testing included evolution through training facilities in the desserts of the Yakima and Fort Irwin training centers, the swamps of Fort Polk in Louisiana, the automated mock urban training centers such as "Leschi Town" at Fort Lewis and "Zussman Village" inside Fort Knox in Kentucky, and even a trip to Korea.

For me the endless amount of training both prolonged the agony of a deployment and strengthened my belief that Deuce Four soldiers would be the best. How could they not be the best, with all the training they had received? What I did not realize until after their boots hit the ground in Iraq, was that soldiers with so much training had to be used in the most dangerous of places. It was inevitable that the thoroughly trained men of Deuce Four would be used to quell the surge of terrorist uprising in one of the most dangerous places of the war – Mosul, Iraq.

As the war continued, the news was full of battlefront coverage. I remember the day I first heard of a city called Mosul in Iraq. My brother had phoned me from Ft. Lewis to talk about the upcoming deployment. There was little news about where they would be going, but his battalion did know that they would be taking over for another brigade from Ft. Lewis that had been deployed for nearly a year in the city of Mosul. I looked at a map and was relieved to find that Mosul was not near Fallujah, Baghdad, Nasiriya, or some of the other cities that had become so familiar through news coverage. What I failed to realize was that as the insurgents were being driven out of the south, they moved north into other cities, including Mosul, and converged with terrorists entering Iraq from the north bordering countries of Syria and Iran. On top of those factions, local residents were joining the fight.

We asked Jon about why so many insurgents were positioned in Mosul during their deployment.

*"The insurgents were mostly people coming from Syria, and were also some of the young kids in the town. There were a bunch of these 19 and 20 year-old kids that in the US would join gangs and things like that. These soldiers from Iran and Syria come in and they basically train these guys. They tell them, 'You can*

37

*be a soldier here, this is how you fire a mortar,this is how you fire a rifle,' and they would give these young people money and weapons, and things like that. And, it was a cool thing to do, especially since the unemployment level is so high there. (An insurgent) walks up to a guy begging on the street and hands him (money) and says, 'here is $500 – go shoot this guy,' how many would actually go and do it? Let me tell you, there would be a lot of them. And if you look at the unemployment level there, which is about 50%, then of course, they are going to start shooting at us."*

When I think about the young, unemployed Iraqis who have been pulled into the terrorists organization, I can't help but think about how closely they resemble the young soldiers in our own Army. While some soldiers enlist because of family tradition, many enter the service for skills training and financial stability. For a lot of enlistees, military service is the first regular, full-time job they have ever had. Without the military, they might be unemployed or underemployed, and susceptible to crooked activities, criminal involvement, or even gang membership.

New recruits come from primarily middle-class families, do not have a college education, and are attracted to the benefits of the G.I. Bill and other college funding available through the military. While 73% of new recruits racially classify themselves as white, there are soldiers of every race and creed in our military. Even though enlistees hail from rural homes more than urban areas, it isn't hard to find soldiers from any big city or small town. The make-up of Deuce Four was diverse, young, and eager for something life at home could not offer them.

As the primary caregiver for my younger brother, who enlisted in the Army through the Delayed Entry Program while still in high school, I took a long time to understand that the life he wanted to lead needed something more than a dead-end job in our hometown could provide. War certainly provided more life experience than I ever wanted for him, but his time in the Army prior to deploying to Iraq gave my brother the chance to travel all over the world, and from that came a lot of excitement and adventure.

The excitement and adventure of military service is not free. Even in wartime, soldiers must provide some of their own supplies and equipment at their own expense. Yes, U.S. soldiers must purchase some of their own equipment for war without reimbursement. It is ridiculous, absurd, and absolutely necessary. About a month before Deuce Four deployed, the men were given a list of items they should have, but would not be provided with, for their time in Iraq. Fortunately, my brother was single and lived on base, so he had funds to cover the cost of the things he needed to buy. Mostly the list was simple: underwear, thermal socks, headlamp or other flashlight, sunglasses, bandannas, and even better boots.

As they packed their gear for Iraq, the soldiers also packed their personal items that would stay on base in storage while they were gone. Our family had concerns about the safety of military storage, so after a trip to the shipping store and $200, most of my brother's valuable items were shipped home to me to store while he was gone. Most of the soldiers received a footlocker for their gear, but the company ran out of footlockers before they were issued to my brother's platoon. The guys were given wood, nails and a saw and told to build their own storage boxes. My brother phoned home during the process of building the footlockers and the scene he described was a spectacle. Somehow, they managed to build the necessary number of footlockers, with only a few minor injuries, and got their gear packed away.

The whole ordeal made me wonder if the military can't seem to get our guys enough footlockers for storage, how could we be sure they would have enough bullets, or food, or medical supplies? We would soon come to learn that the supply chain to our war bound soldiers had more than a few kinks.

---

*I recall the period between January 2004 and October 2004, with some fuzziness. I remember having a nagging, irresolvable worry that the unit to which Jon was assigned, Deuce Four, would be sent to Iraq. We thought soon, but never quite knew when. First, it would be early in 2004, then, May of 2004, then, a new leader was assigned and there was some rule about having a certain amount of training experience with the unit that had to be satisfied. It just seemed to go on and on. Would we see Jon again before he deployed? No....yes....maybe...yes. In these days, I was learning the Army ways, and found it frustrating.*

*My husband, who served in the Army in the Vietnam era, seemed to take it all in stride – which sometimes confused and upset me. I guess not everything about the "New Army" has changed. The "hurry up and wait" and "no news is good news" phenomena continue to be true. Tom had already been "hammered" into acceptance of this as normal, and I was still adjusting to the ways of the military life.*

*Since we were in Arizona and Jon was stationed at Ft. Lewis, Washington, we heard from Jon infrequently.*

*Generally, the conversations would revolve around the last time Jon and his friends rented a room together and partied off base, or the latest things Jon was involved in for training and deployment preparations. For example, being the medical person involved in a training exercise. Jon said that he usually participated in the exercise as much as he could, at least until someone sprained an ankle or something that required his Medic skills. He thought it was important that his new group - the Infantry guys - have respect for him not just as their "doc" but also as an able soldier. These are definitely my words, not Jon's. He would have said something more like, "I don't want them to think I'm a lard ass."*

*Always threaded in the conversations were the latest in a series of careless overspending or bounced checks. All three of our sons have referred to their mother as "Banco de Mama". This means when they would have a spending deficit, they would run to "Banco de Mama", who would issue an emergency loan. They were always expected to repay Mama - interest free - in either cash or trade.*

41

*As I look back on it, I now realize Jon's usual bad spending habits grew increasingly reckless as deployment approached. The culminating example was shortly before he left for Iraq. He bought a car, through a sleazy credit company, at an outrageous interest rate. We, the parents, were only told about this AFTER the event, so there was nothing we could do to change that bad decision. His logic for the purchase was that the car would be safely guarded at the Ft. Lewis storage lot during the deployment, and would be "nearly paid for" by the time he returned. We could just hear the fast talking used car salesman's spiel in our son's explanation. The naiveté of the majority of our young service men and women is astounding, and the willingness of "patriotic" Americans to swindle them is unbelievable.*

*Jon did manage to save enough money while at Ft. Lewis to buy a laptop computer. He proudly told us that he was allowed to use it for keeping track of the men's immunization record collection - and it was much faster and easier to use than the military equipment available.*

*Apparently, he also let some of the soldiers in his company use the computer, which led to an unfortunate, but also comical event involving our whole family. By the time this event occurred, Jon already had Yahoo Instant Messenger loaded onto his laptop, and we all had him as a friend, in our contact lists. Whenever Jon would log on to his computer we would see him. Jon paid for his own internet service to his room in his barracks. Anyway, Jon left his laptop turned on one day, in his room, so that it could be used by a friend. He told the friend to lock up the room when he was finished, because he had to leave for some*

42

*duty. Jon learned that was a bad move. NEVER leave your personal items without locking them up in the barracks. When Jon returned, the laptop was gone. He contacted us and we contacted the Company Commander. Before we knew it, the barracks were on lock down. Tom, a veteran, was much more familiar with chain of command, who to call, etc. and he set to work investigating by phone. It was not long until Tom had the time frame nailed down and who was on duty in HQ at the time of the theft. The noose was beginning to tighten. Jon, was not too happy about all this for many reasons. His comrades were pretty upset about being on lock down. For a while, no one would fess up to anything and everyone was confined to quarters. THEN, out of the blue, our son, Tommy, Jon's older brother, heard the Yahoo knock-knock of Jon's computer online. He immediately sent a barrage of questions to the person using Jon's computer. Tommy asked him how he could live with himself after stealing from a soldier about to deploy to Iraq, and used language that was never fully divulged to me, his mother. OBVIOUSLY, the story of the laptop thief was that he was about two times removed from the original thief, and had bought Jon's computer thinking he was getting a "smoking hot" deal. Fortunately, the thief with Jon's computer was also a computer novice. Before it was over, my son Tommy and husband Tom had the thief convinced that they knew exactly where he and the computer were located from his IP address, and that the military and local police would be at his door in minutes. They warned him to make his life easier by going immediately to the Deuce Four HQ and return the computer. Believe it or not, the computer was returned!*

*We don't really know exactly who stole the computer, or what happened after that, but Jon got his laptop back, and the torturous lock down was lifted. A short time later Jon left for Iraq with the laptop, though it did not weather the trip well and was broken when he arrived. More importantly, Jon left knowing that his family would do whatever it took to cover his back while he was in Iraq. I believe this knowledge was far more valuable than any other thing that Jon could have had with him at war.*

## SNEAK ATTACK

On December 21, 2004, a suicide bomber dressed as an Iraqi soldier snuck into the mess tent at FOB Marez and detonated a bomb. Fourteen American soldiers and eight civilians were killed in the attack, and 69 others were wounded. An insurgent group known as Jaish Ansar al-Sunna claimed responsibility for the attack. It was the deadliest attack on US soldiers since the war in Iraq began.

During a visit home in December 2008, Patti asked Jon how the soldiers reacted to the Mess Hall Attack.

*"We all were very, very upset," Jon told us. "They hit us...really it was like a cheap shot. It was like someone walking down the mall and someone just punching you while you are holding your baby or something...they hit us where we were not expecting it. We were all very upset the day it hit us and by the mass confusion that followed. I mean you had commanders that were injured, killed in our case, and you know a lot of your friends, the ones that had died and the ones that were critically injured that you're not sure how bad it really is. And, not just that but now we're completely isolated because you will not have phone privileges or internet access at all until everyone's located and everyone's family is told about it. You are completely cut off with your support back home, with everyone except your immediate soldiers...well, family there...it*

*was really an eye opener. I guess until that point we really had thought that, you know, it wasn't that bad there. Yes, they were shooting at us, but it was almost like a game of paint ball."*

On the morning of December 21st I had decided to get away from the television and I went to town. I finished my Christmas shopping, bought groceries and tried to run as many errands as possible just to get them out of the way. It felt refreshing to be away from the computer and the television. I did not return home until late in the afternoon.

When I arrived home, my phone rang. It was Patti phoning to ask if I was okay and had I heard any news. I was bewildered. "Why?" I asked. "Has something happened?" I turned on the television and found the answer to my questions. I just could not believe what I was seeing.

For those of us back home, the attack was a shock whose sting would not go away. We tried hard to comfort each other while we waited for word whether our soldiers were dead or alive.

*IM – Patti & Jenn on the evening of December 21, 2004*

*Patti: Hi Jenn - made it home. Had dinner...now waiting for news to roll around to Mosul*

*Jenn: I have been trying to keep myself busy*

*Patti: This is terrible isn't it.*

*Jenn: It's just the worst since they left...the not knowing.*

46

*Jenn: It would be horrible to be at Ft. Lewis during all this, you know?*

*Patti: Yes - I am sure. I have not checked the news services in about 2 hours - nothing new?*

*Jenn: I haven't seen anything new - a couple of additional photos, but no news*

*Patti:I figured. CNN is doing a big story on the incident after Larry King.*

*Jenn: What time is that? 10pm EST*

*Patti: Not sure - I would guess so - seems like the current discussion is about to wrap up - that would be about 13 min from now.*

*Jenn: I'm going to watch that*

*Patti: me too*

*Jenn: on the NBC nightly news there were a couple of reporters that had been in the dining hall, that was pretty hard to listen to*

*Patti: I didn't see that*

*Jenn: Well, I was making dinner when it was on, so I watched it again on the MSNBC website*

*Patti: What did they say?*

*Jenn: I tried really hard not to get upset in front of my 8 year-old, that didn't work out so well, so we made tacos and turned off the TV and turned on some Christmas music to make us feel better*

*Patti: Oh - that must have been really hard for you, but it is a good thing we have to be strong for our loved ones or we would just crack up totally.*

*Jenn: I know - I never wanted to be one of those 'strong women', but sometimes you just don't get to decide*

*Patti: Yes - that is true. God doesn't give us more than we can handle, but, sometimes He gets REALLY close to the limit.*

*Jenn: I just keep telling myself that no news is good news.*

*Patti: YES - and we know that is true.*

*Jenn: I sent James an IM so when he logs on it will be the first thing he sees*

*Patti: Good idea - I will do the same.*

*Jenn: If he logs on in the middle of the night I won't be up probably, but I wanted him to know I was thinking about them*

*Patti: Yes - they will probably try to contact us as soon as they are allowed.*

*Jenn: Thanks for the heads up about CNN - I'm going to watch right now*

*Patti: OK - hope we have the time right - see you later.*

*Jenn: ttyl, and thanks for being so good to me*

*Patti: Oh my goodness...it is me who should be thanking you. Bye for now.*

That night seemed to last forever. I absolutely could not sleep. Every headlight that flashed through the windows as cars drove down our street made our hearts jump. Would this car turn into our driveway? Would soldiers knock on my door to tell me the unthinkable?

Thousands of miles away at Ft. Lewis, soldiers' wives were holding vigil as well. Everyone was staying home, close to the phone and internet, praying their soldier would make contact to let them know they had survived the attack. The waiting was excruciating.

The FRG did their best to keep us posted. In the afternoon, we received an email from Honey Bartel, our main contact with the support group.

*Hi All,*

*I'm sure most of you are watching CNN right now wondering the FRG knows anything at all. Unfortunately, the answer to that question is no. We are getting our information from CNN also.*

*Please keep in mind that after any kind of incident the Army shuts down all phones and email centers on the FOB until after ALL official casualty notifications have occurred.*

*Also, should your loved one call you and tell you that he has been injured, please remember that unless you call the POC the FRG will not know of your situation.*

*Let's try and remain positive that our loved ones are fine and will contact us as soon as they are able. Be strong.*

*Take care,*

*Honey*

While the email didn't relay any bad news, we could all see the images on television. I remember a photograph taken inside the mess hall that showed soldiers with stretchers carrying out the wounded. The insignia on their uniforms was clearly that of Deuce Four. We all knew that we had reason to worry. Later in the evening we received another email from the FRG, this time sent from Riikka Jacobsen, the wife of the A-Company commander.

*Ladies,*

*Honey and I have received many phone calls all day today and I wanted to send you this email letting you know that we really don't know anything yet. As soon as we hear something we will let you know. We are all following CNN and hope to hear something soon.*

*If you do get a phone call and your husband has been injured, please do call... because otherwise we won't know and will not be able to help you. Please, be strong. We keep praying for all of our guys out there.*

## Riikka

The email helped pick me up and reminded me to be strong. As each hour passed with no one phoning me or knocking on my door, I felt more encouraged that my brother was not among the dozens CNN was reporting as wounded or killed. I also felt selfish because I knew someone was opening their door to the worst news possible. It was horrific.

Around midnight a third email came through. The memo read, "No News Yet", and this time it was sent by Honey, not Riikka. I knew even before reading it that the waiting was not over.

*Everyone,*

*At this time, neither Riikka nor I have heard anything regarding any casualties in A Co 1-24. As soon as we hear something, we will let you know. If you hear from your soldier please contact us.*

*As always, no news is good news...and yes, I know, that doesn't help and waiting sucks.*

*Be strong.*

*Honey*

The night went on and on, but we began to feel that since we had not received any notification that our soldiers were okay. Still, there was no news. The only instant messages were from other loved ones offering support and looking for news. Getting through December 21ˢᵗ was one of the biggest challenges for all of us.

Once we got past 10:00pm, many families began to breathe a little easier. Notification is normally made only between 8am and 10pm local time. However, because the mess hall attack was so catastrophic in the shear number of casualties, notification continued until it was complete, well after 10pm.

A soldier's next of kin, or NOK, is notified in person of their death by a Casualty Notification Officer. This visit is made as inconspicuously as possible, so as not to draw attention to the family during such a time of tragedy. Every unknown car entering my neighborhood became 'that' car – the one that would find me with horrible news.

Once the door is answered, the Casualty Notification Officers identifies themselves...

*"I am Captain..."*

*"Are you the mother of..."*

*"I have an important message to deliver from the Secretary of the Army, may I come in?"*

*"The Secretary of the Army has asked me to express his deep regret that..."*

The process is completely scripted. The role of the Casualty Notification Officer must be difficult. Despite the lack of personal danger, it is the role of CNO in war that no soldier can envy, because the faces of the next of kin will forever live in their hearts and minds. The CNO is ordered to memorize the script, deliver the message without hurry or gruesome details, to not touch the NOK unless they are in shock or faint, and to leave the residence as soon as possible.

*"I must return to the base. Again, on behalf of the Secretary of the Army, please accept the United States Army's deepest condolences."*

It was those cold words, delivered in a strange car by an unknown soldier, that we all feared the most. At 10:02 pm, Honey received an email from Riikka, simply saying, "We made it. I'm going to bed."

After reading the email, Honey picked up the phone and immediately phoned Riikka the share some thoughts before bed. Five minutes later, at 10:07 pm, while talking with Honey, Riikka heard a knock on her door. With Honey still on the phone line, Riikka answered the door and overheard a man say, "Are you the wife of Captain William Jacobsen?" And then, Honey heard the phone drop to the floor. Within the hour, Riikka's cherished friends and neighbors, including Honey, gathered in her home to offer what little comfort they could to help ease Riikka's grief.

The evening of December 22<sup>nd</sup> Mary Paige Kurilla, the wife of the Deuce Four Commander, Lieutenant Colonel Erik Kurilla, forwarded an email from her husband to the families of Deuce Four. Each time a soldier in the brigade was killed or severely wounded, the families back home would receive an email from the Commander. This email was different. The casualties from the mess hall attack were in the dozens. The attack itself was unfathomable; reading the email from the Deuce Four Commander was gut wrenching. Not only had A-Company lost it's commander, Captain Bill Jacobsen, but it had also lost Sergeant Robert Johnson, and two engineers, Specialist Jonathan Castro and Private Lionel Ayro. Additionally, twenty-four Deuce Four soldiers were wounded in the attack; seven so severely that they were evacuated to the military hospital in Landstuhl, Germany. Many other soldiers were returned to duty with light wounds. They all were deeply grieving. As were we.

Because notification of next of kin was still on-going, the Commander did not list the names in his email. The blackout on communications was lifted, but the remaining soldiers were out on combat missions. It was excruciating waiting to hear the news. We would either receive a phone call or email from our soldiers letting us know they survived, or we would receive the dreadful visit from the Casualty Notification Officer that we all so deeply feared.

It was two days before we had the chance to chat with our soldiers. While we were relieved that our boys were safe, Patti and I each felt sorrow for the other families and guilt for the 'happiness' we felt. Our boys were safe, so we rejoiced. Knowing how many other families were in

despair made me feel shameful. How could I be so happy?
Would I feel the sorrow of losing my brother?

At lunchtime on December 21st my brother parked his
Stryker just outside the mess entrance along with several
other Strykers, all having just returned from missions
'outside the wire'. The group of soldiers walked toward
the tent for what they expected to be a normal lunch.
James planned to sit near his friend, Jon Castro, other men
in A-Company, and Captain Jacobsen, just like every other
meal in the mess hall. Another soldier told James he heard
there was cake and he wanted to get a couple of pieces
before they ran out. My brother asked his friend to grab an
extra piece of cake for him. As James walked toward the
hand-washing station a few feet away from the entrance to
the tent, when the explosion happened.

*"It was the loudest noise I ever heard," James recalled.
"I thought maybe it was a rocket attack or something
because we had been having a lot of those. Then I saw
that everything was all blown up...the tables were all
over the place and guys were laying around everywhere
hurt and bleeding. Some of the chairs looked like they
were run over by a truck or something and this was all
mixed with the food trays and everything was all
smoky. People were screaming and running around and
there were some guys in the National Guard just
standing around like they were in shock or something.
It was crazy...just like chaos everywhere. A lot of our
guys started taking off shirts and jackets to use them*

*to try to help the wounded because there were guys bleeding all over.*

*At first, I was just thinking how I can't believe this happened, like it was a movie or something. There was a guy, he was still in his chair at a lunch table, and he was slumped over his tray, and the back of his head was just blown up. I just stood there and couldn't believe it, then one of our sergeants came over and put his fleece (jacket) over the guy's head and then he said we needed to help people get out of there, so then I just became a robot. We started out using litters, which means stretcher, and carrying out the wounded, but there weren't anymore litters so we just started carrying out people right on the tables. There was just food and blood and body parts everywhere, all over the floor, making it slippery, and we were walking all in it just to get to people. Some guys were working on Captain J, and doing CPR I think, then they took him out on a stretcher, but he died on the way to the hospital. That just was hard to make sense of because he was just sitting at our table with our guys and then everything blew up and he was gone.*

*The inside of the tent, which was our mess hall, was just wrecked up and there was a big hole in the top of it. Some of the tables had been blown around by the explosion and they were melted to the walls. That was real bad because some guys were trapped under these melted tables and we were trying to pry the tables off of them, and there is just all this food and dead bodies everywhere and everything is all burned up and it's hard to talk about, you know? And my friend Jon Castro died in there. That's whose name is on my bracelet, on my memorial bracelet. We all got them while we were still over there and I got one with him because he was just my really good friend. I went down with him to his house in California for Thanksgiving one time and that was great. I was going to go back there sometime after the war, you know..."*

Dealing with the trauma that he witnessed that day, and other days while in Iraq, has been difficult for my brother. He lost a leader and he lost brothers; brothers who will always be his friends for life.

*IM with Jenn and James, December 24, 2004*

*James: Hi Jenn*

*Jenn: Are you okay? I've been worried about you & Jon*

*James: Yeah I'm fine so is Jon, he wasn't at the FOB*

*Jenn: SOOO good to hear – I'll tell Jon's mom...I'm sorry for the losses in Deuce Four, where were you?*

*James: I was walking in when it went off*

*Jenn: Oh my, were you close*

*James: About 30 ft away*

*Jenn: You are so lucky - the pictures on TV are awful*

*James: Yeah...I helped patch people up*

*Jenn: Many people have been calling here to see about you - I'm really proud of you and thankful to God for your safety*

*James: Yeah I helped about 4 people*

*Jenn: How did you help? Were they people you know?*

*James: By helping them stop bleeding, and yes, I knew them, some of my friends and our Commander died*

*Jenn: I'm so sorry for you, and I'm sorry for their parents and families, I heard about CPT Jacobsen, his wife Riikka was one of the POC/FRG*

*James: Yeah that was our CO*

*Jenn: You've been working a lot since then, haven't you*

*James: Yep*

*Jenn: That has to be really hard to see your friends like that*

*James: I didn't need that - I got blood all over my pants*

*Jenn: Oh no that's awful James, I'm so sorry for you, I want to give you a really big long hug - I saw the Deuce Four arm patches on the news in the mess hall and knew right away that you guys were in there*

*James: Yeah, I went inside when it first went off*

*Jenn: I'm hurting for the families, but I'm so much better knowing that you are okay, I haven't slept more than 1-2 hours since Tuesday*

*James: I was knocked down and my ears hurt it was so loud, it was a big blast*

*Jenn: I'm thanking God right now for saving your life*

*James: 2 minutes later I would have been sitting down*

*Jenn: I've got like 20 people to call today and tell them that you are okay - yesterday the phone just rang off the hook*

*James: Who?*

*Jenn: People from church, friends from work, the neighbors - you name it, I think anyone that didn't call was afraid that you might have been a casualty, I feel like I just got the best Christmas present*

*James: Me too, but we helped a lot of people*

*Jenn: The news has been saying how the Strykers from Ft Lewis were really hard hit and that's got people scared -- they know that is you...the neighbors said that they didn't want to ask, but they didn't want to not ask, you know? The church is running a prayer chain for your wounded*

*James: Prayer is working*

*Jenn: I'll tell them!*

*James: I got lucky*

*Jenn: I think being lucky is really just being blessed. The news has been praising the efforts of soldiers on the* scene, *they said you guys saved a lot of lives, they said you turned over tables and used them as stretchers*

*James: We did, I think if we weren't there then more people would have died because some of the POGS were just standing around in shock*

*Jenn: What are POGS?*

*James: People Other than Grunts, non-combat soldiers*

*Jenn: Oh yeah, I bet they were really terrified*

*James: They didn't know what to do. I was like that at first, and then I went to work on people*

*Jenn: Who was your friend that died*

*James: Jon Castro*

*Jenn: I'll pray for his family...*

*James: We ran out of bandages and we were using napkins and ace bandages*

*Jenn: How many people were wounded? All the news channels say different things*

*James: Lots, you wouldn't believe it...when I first went in there – just carnage - lots of people screaming, a lot of civilians, too, and I think all of the Filipino cooks were killed, I wasn't ready to see that kind of stuff, like people's heads blown up*

*Jenn: I know there isn't anything I can do for you, but I wish I could make you feel better, make this go away*

*James: I think I'm not going to forget about it*

*Jenn: No you won't - just live your best life because it's a great gift from God*

*Jenn:  Grant's coming online to talk to you - he has cried for you some these past days*

*James: Did you tell him?*

*Jenn: Yeah and it was all over TV, I mean every channel had this on...pictures, interviews, consultants, so he saw me watching... it's hard here when we don't know and every time the phone rang I got nervous...the FedEx man came yesterday afternoon in a plain gray van and I got scared when I saw him, too*

*James: I'm sorry about that*

*Jenn: You don't need to be sorry it's just part of it - being here back home*

*James: I bet*

*Jenn: I just kept praying the whole time*

*James: I'm okay, I'm tough, I hope I proved that*

*Jenn: You are the toughest!*

*Jenn: When are they going to get you guys some food? Do you have MREs?*

*James: I've been eating Ramen noodles thanks to you Jenn...well I have to go*

*Jenn: Okay I'm really glad to hear from you luv u*

*James: Love you too Jenn, tell Grant and dad that too*

*Jenn: I will, and they know! We all love you and you are so brave*

*James: OK bye Jenn*

The news was mixed. Our boys were safe, but others were lost and the effects of that horrible day would live on with our soldiers forever.

---

*December 22, 2004, was my 27<sup>th</sup> Wedding Anniversary with my husband Tom. A momentous day, one would think. This anniversary was momentous in a different way and it was well into January before we realized that our anniversary had past. Strange.*

*I was at work the 21<sup>st</sup> of December, when Tom called me to alert me to the news reports. A mess tent had been attacked in Mosul. By this time, Jenn and I had become "war buddies". I dialed her cell phone, and asked if she had seen the news. She had not. Earlier that day Jenn decided to take a break from her incessant Iraq news report watching to do some Christmas shopping.*

*The hardest thing about this event was the waiting. It was Christmas Eve before the communication "Black Out" between the Deuce Four soldiers and their families was lifted as all the families of the casualties were notified. Normally this notification takes about 24 hours, but due to the very large number of dead and wounded, notification took longer.*

*We waited nervously. Every car that entered our driveway was quickly scanned for the military car look - black walls, plain look, two soldiers dressed in green. We prayed that our son had been spared. I caught myself praying that some other mother's son had been killed, and then cried that I could be so callous. It was a horror. And, it set the stage for the rest of the deployment.*

*We learned that this horrific blast, which killed Captain Jacobsen, beloved leader of A-Company, Deuce Four, our son's company, had been caused by a suicide insurgent that breached security entering the FOB dressed as an Iraqi soldier, with explosives. HOW COULD THIS HAPPEN!? How could security be so low on FOB Marez to allow this to occur?*

*IM – Patti, husband Tom & Jon, December 24, 2004*

*Jon:   Hey there Mom, just wanted to talk to you to tell you that I am okay.*

*Patti: JON – thank GOD – we heard you were OK – but sure glad to see you online. Can you talk awhile?*

*Jon:   Yes*

*Patti: I am going to conference your Dad into the chat*

*Jon:   I got lucky...I had a 24-hour guard duty that was outside the wire so I didn't see anything.*

*Tom:Hi son, love you*

*Jon:   Hello there Dad*

*Tom: We have been going nuts here worrying. What mission were you on?*

63

*Jon:* I had guard duty outside the wire so I was about a mile or two away.

*Tom:* We heard that your Captain was killed.

*Jon:* Yeah, it sounded bad. I am helping with the aftermath, re-dressing wounds and stuff.

*Tom:* James said he was just going into the mess hall when the bomb went off.

*Jon:* Yeah he was washing his hands.

*Tom:* Wow! Our prayers were answered again.

*Jon:* There were stainless steel tables in there and the bomb was so strong that they were peeling the metal tables off the wall to un-stick people.

*Patti:* Do you have food? James said many were hungry there.

*Jon:* We have some food, but they haven't really planned things for that kind of hit to our mess hall

*Tom:* How are things with the troop as far as morale goes?

*Jon:* It is very low, as you might imagine.

*Tom:* Was it your Captain that got killed, Jon?

*Jon:* Yes, and we had some close friends die.

*Patti:* Your whole family has been holding it's breath, so to speak, for the last 3 days.

*Jon:    I have to say that I am really lucky I guess because I normally eat at the same table as Captain J.*

*Patti:You are blessed son.*

*Jon:    The night before I left I had a long conversation with him (Captain J.)*

*Patti:What was it about?*

*Jon:    We were eating together at this little Hajji restaurant, and we were just talking about how effective we have been over the last month. He was a really caring man and very upbeat.*

*Patti: Your good strong attitude and belief in the Lord will help those that survived.*

*Tom:It has to be rough on all the men.*

*Patti: Be happy, be strong…you are in a wonderful position to help people find Jesus.*

*Jon:    One can only hope*

*Patti: Was the bomber seated at the same table as your Captain?*

*Jon:    No…they aren't too sure that it was a bomber like that..I am looking at where the bomb went off and no one ever sits there. There were a bunch of tables in there with sheets over them, so a bomb could have been placed underneath them. That's where I have heard the bomb went off.*

*Tom: The news said that it was an Iraqi man who was working for 2 months on the base. That he had a bag with a bomb in it and he just walked in and detonated it.*

*Jon: No one is allowed in the mess hall with a bag, so that is hard to believe unless someone screwed up*

*Patti: How many were actually hurt...from your viewpoint?*

*Jon: 83 casualties, two today just dressing changes, and 23 I have heard now dead*

*Patti: Oh, terrible news, another died*

*Tom: Sounds like security needs to be beefed up.*

*Jon:     Well, I am guessing that the General that is in charge of security is going to beef it up after he removes the boot from his ass*

*Tom: You are probably right*

*Jon:     Well, this is info from the aid station so it isn't confirmed yet, but one of the first lieutenants punched out a reporter that was in the way and he was trying to interview guys that were bandaging up people. I can't say that I blame him, though.*

*Tom: The Lt. Colonel's letter that he sent out to the families of soldiers in A-Company was pretty sad*

*Patti: Well, too bad for the reporters...they have to stay out of the way. Jon, please tell me if you are OK with FOOD*

*Jon:     I am doing fine here. I am going to the memorial ceremony tomorrow. I knew that it was bad when I saw the Lt. Colonel with red eyes after it happened.*

*Tom: What kind of injuries have you been treating?*

*Jon:     Just small stuff for the people that have been returned to duty.*

*Patti: You are going to a ceremony for the guys that died?*

*Tom: I didn't think they would have that yet?*

*Jon:     Well, we have to send the bodies home.*

*Patti: It is good to have some grieving time.*

*Tom: How is your attitude, Jon?*

*Jon:     Well, it has been better*

*Tom: You have to stop and get your attitude back up so you can have the Lord work through you son. We love you so much.*

*Jon:     That is so important*

*Patti: Did you see the instant messages that Dad & I left for you when you signed on*

*Jon:     Yes, I sent you guys a message hoping that you guys would see it.*

*Patti: GOOD – you can instant message or text my phone anytime. That way, we will know you are okay.*

*Jon:     Well, James said that he let you guys know that I was alive so that took a load off of me. I was thinking that we wouldn't be able to call until after Christmas. We had to re-load and then run to the truck.*

*Tom: Where did you go after reloading...to guard bridges?*

*Jon:     No, we drove around for a while looking for trouble and then I've been trying to get medical supplies*

*Patti: The news said most were not wearing any body armor. Do you wear your armor when you eat?*

*Jon: No. That wasn't a real problem before. The mortars they've been firing were too far away to hit the mess hall. As well, the bullets wouldn't be effective.*

*Patti:  WELL, I hope you will change your practices now, since it is obvious that the FOB has been compromised. If there was one infiltrator there are probably more.*

*Jon:     Well, we will see. I am sure that things will get really stupid here for a while. Every Iraqi personnel has been fired.*

*Patti: The enemy is very cunning son...you must come home to us*

*Jon:    We are doing everything we can... I am doing everything I can*

*Patti: We heard that they will try to have the mess tent repaired for Christmas...have you heard anything like that?*

*Jon:    That isn't going to happen, not with the damage*

*Patti: I think they should use Air Force One to cater in dinner for you guys*

*Jon:    That would be nice*

*Patti: Do you need us to send anything?*

*Jon:    Send jerky and some Ramen noodle cups*

*Patti: Okay – you got it. We are worried about you guys having the basic supplies and food you need. Do you have any food left from the last box that we sent?*

*Jon:    Yes, thankfully I have some, but it is running out quickly. MREs get old fast.*

*Patti: YES, I imagine that they do, but glad you are getting them. You should know that everybody has been sending emails and praying for you guys constantly.*

*Jon:    That is good. The guys here jumped into action. They were the main effort that helped all of the people.*

*Patti: You mean your company?*

*Jon:  Yes, the rest of the Reserves and National Guard here were just standing around*

*Patti: Well they are not as well trained, probably were in shock.*

*Jon:  Yeah, but there were National Guard medics that ran into the mess hall and then ran right back out because they freaked out. Our guys grabbed their medic bags and took them in while the National Guard sat there crying*

*Patti: Oh boy, well...thank God you had your guys well trained to step in.*

*Jon:  I am glad – a lot more would have died*

*Patti: GOOD lesson in how important it is for everyone to have first aid training. You never know who is going to buckle under stress.*

*Jon:  I got two packages today from our cousins in Ohio*

*Patti: YUMM – I bet there was some good stuff in there*

*Jon:  Yeah, but I gave some beef to RPG*

*Patti: What is RPG?*

*Jon:  RPG is the kitten's name here. Can you send me some de-wormer?*

*Patti: You mean you are feeding a kitten?*

*Jon:* *Yeah, some guys are keeping the kitten in their room but we ran out of food for it. Hey, I am going to get off of here so others can get word home. I love you mom.*

*Patti: OK SON – please try to get back on soon – we have not been sleeping too well – LOVE YOU SO MUCH – BE CAREFUL – KEEP BODY ARMOR ON AT ALL TIMES – that is an ORDER*

*Jon:* *Okay, love you all, ttyl*

*Patti: XXXOOO – love and prayers your way*

*\*Jon has left the conversation\**

At the same time, we were able to have a chat with Derek Young, another driver in 3$^{rd}$ platoon.

*IM- Patti and Derek, December 24, 2004, Christmas Eve*

*Derek: Hello, how are you?*

*Patti: Hello Derek! GREAT – now that we know you guys are OK*

*Derek: Yeah, I know my parents were worried too and so was my fiancée*

*Patti: Do you talk with them online? If so, feel free to give them my IM contact.*

*Derek: Okay, I will do that*

*Patti: We are able to communicate with James' sister and it really helps. Where are you from?*

71

*Derek: North Carolina*

*Patti: Nice state... what is your job?*

*Derek: I drive the Stryker*

*Patti: GOOD – stay inside and close to my Jon – I know you guys watch out for each other*

*Derek: Yeah we do, and I will, believe me*

*Patti: GOOD – he is a good son, nice person, and I need him around to make my grandchildren someday*

*Derek: My fiancée would kill me and Jon if anything happened to either one of us*

*Patti: Stay on guard and keep that body armor on – I don't care how long you have to wear it – only take it off for the shower*

*Derek: I will, I promise*

*Patti: What do you guys need? I am working on another box to send*

*Derek: You don't have to do that*

*Patti: I know, I want to*

*Derek: Okay, you talked me into it then, Jerky and snacks*

*Patti: Our family has the goal of taking really GOOD care of 3rd Platoon. You guys are closer than brothers right now.*

*Derek: Yes, I think we are*

*Patti: We are all praying for you, constantly. You have no idea how many people are praying..It is quite amazing*

*Derek: Thanks, we need it. I know I have a whole ward praying for me at Ft. Lewis*

*Patti: It is protecting you. How amazing that 3rd platoon was shielded.*

*Derek: Yep, we are truly blessed.*

*Patti: Well, the Lord must have plans for you – I know you and Jon are trying to be good examples – have good attitudes and bring more souls to Jesus. You are in the perfect place for attracting people with open hearts. The Lord protects his soldiers*

*Derek: Yes HE does. I have to go, ttyl – much love to you guys*

*Patti: Okay, thanks for the chat – prayers for you – take care*

*Any sense of trust in our soldiers being safe on the FOB disappeared. There was no moment of our soldiers' day, which was many hours ahead of our day, that we could have any sense that they were OK. I thank God our son was on a mission that horrible day rather than at the FOB having lunch lured into the idea that he was safe there.*

*As the rest of the United States quickly forgot those dead soldiers, Tom and I learned to live with a higher level of concern for the Stryker Brigade and especially for our son and his platoon-mates. Our Anniversary, Dec 22<sup>nd</sup> was lost; Christmas 2004 and New Years 2005 were a blur of time. Between the higher security immediately imposed on the FOB and the critical role that the Brigade played in preparing and providing security for the first Elections in Iraq, January 30, 2005, our contacts with Jon were few. We did not fully realize it at the time, but we were entering a difficult period for the next five months.*

*On the brighter side, Jenn and I were there for each other that day and the days that followed. Our friendship grew steadily as we waited together, or in shifts, for our soldiers to appear online.*

# REMEMBERING CAPTAIN J

On December 21, 2004, A-Company Captain William W. Jacobsen Jr., 31, died when a suicide bomber attacked the mess hall at FOB Marez. To all the soldiers of A-Company, Captain J will always be their leader. He was personable and honorable; a fine man who was completely approachable.

*My son Jon had this to say about his leader:*

*"CPT Jacobsen was just an amazing guy. He was one of the officers that took the time to actually talk to his soldiers. Most of the officers just viewed you as like second class, almost. But, he would come down and just talk to you. I remember one of the times Derek Young and myself, we were both at this little "Hajji" eatery that was on the FOB. This was a couple of days before his death. Captain J was waiting for some type of chicken meal it took them a long time to cook it. And he sat down and just wanted to know what we thought of the guard rotation through the tower, or one of the COPS, which was the Command Operation Post that was out in the city that we had to sit on. He actually listened to us. He would talk to us on an individual level, which made us feel a lot better. It made it seem like he really cared. Before we deployed, he actually brought his kids over to the unit and I remember numerous times his children just running around and*

75

*getting into mischief and things like that. He was a*
*REAL guy....not a boss or a commander, but a real*
*person that we all respected."*

*Honey Bartel's recollection of the high level of respect and love*
*that her husband, MSG Matt Bartel had for CPT Jacobsen was*
*inspiring. Even though CPT Van Antwerp was assigned to his*
*duties after the tragedy of Captain J's death, all the men still*
*considered Captain J their real captain.*

*Captain J left behind his wife, Riikka, four children, both of his*
*parents, and 184 Stryker Brigade, A-Company soldiers. His*
*passing was truly mourned.*

*For the many soldiers he led, Bill Jacobsen is their hero. He*
*trained them. He inspired them to be great warriors. He prepared*
*them for deployment and was with them every step of the way.*
*He respected and loved them. He even woke them up to the true*
*level of danger they faced in Mosul through his death that awful*
*day in the mess tent. Captain J knew how to lead the most*
*effective way, not by demanding respect, but by deserving and*
*earning respect from each of his soldiers. He continues to inspire*
*his family and his soldiers today. In that way, he still lives on in*
*their hearts.*

# OUR BOYS ARE HUNGRY

By Christmas Eve 2004, Patti and I had both received word that our boys, Jon and James survived the mess hall attack. Although comforting, we still felt the painful loss of so many comrades and friends.

An unexpected after-effect of the mess hall attack was that the food service for FOB Marez completely shut down. Our sleep deprived, devastated, exhausted soldiers were now famished on top of everything else.

*IM – Patti and Jenn, December 24, 2004*

*Patti: Good morning, Jenn. I hope you got some sleep.*

*Jenn: Yes, I tried. I do feel rested and I'm trying to get in the Christmas spirit. How are you doing?*

*Patti: Pretty good. Had a little low feeling this morning - looking at Rumsfeld on TV - visiting Mosul. Great looking breakfast they were having, a cellophane wrapped "egg mc-muffin" looking thing. If that is what they are serving him, can you imagine what Jon and James are getting?*

*Jenn: That is exactly what I was thinking – disgusts me. They probably flew that food into Iraq with Rumsfeld.*

*Patti: Must be a "MOM" thing to think. I don't know...just feeling guilty when I eat anything, knowing what they are going through...sure hope it lasts a while, I could use some weight loss to counteract all the "pacification" eating I have done the past few months.*

*Jenn: I was baking last night for Christmas, and I felt the same way. I did make 2 banana breads for the boys and I'm hoping to mail those today.*

*Patti: I have some cookies to send. Is post office open today? It is Christmas Eve, so I don't know if they are open. Is that how you send your packages, via USPS?*

*Jenn: I send all my packages US Postal Service. They are open today until 2pm. I froze the banana breads right after I baked them and today I'm going to vacuum seal them in the food saver, so I'm hoping they will arrive fairly fresh.*

*Patti: I think your banana bread will be fine - we use the vacuum sealer too - for stuff we send. I just sent a dozen Christmas cookies to Jon.*

*Patti: Do you have any of the other soldiers on your contact list so you know when James' friends are online?*

*Jenn: No, James and Ashley's instant message IDs are the only ones I know*

*Patti: We now have Jon, James, Ashley and Derek. Let me send you Jon and Derek's screen names. You can add them to your instant message list - just tell them you are James' sister and they will accept you, I am sure.*

*Jenn: That will be great - and thank you for sending me a copy of the conversation you had with James– that was really nice of you and a great idea.*

*Patti: GREAT! Believe it or not, I get a lot of information that I didn't think to ask from your conversations and email you have forwarded. Honey is now sending email to us...that is a GREAT help!*

*Jenn: I thanked Honey yesterday for all the information she sends- even when it wasn't anything more than prayers. It's just nice to have communication.*

*Patti: Jon told Ashley yesterday that he will be on a mission through Christmas and we should not expect to hear from him until Sunday. I don't know which guys he is with...so that may not be true for James.*

*Jenn: Well, I'm logging off now, I'll probably be back on later, but if I don't talk to you, I hope you have a very merry Christmas and God bless you!*

*Patti: Thanks & have a great day & a wonderful holiday. Love to all of you.*

More than two weeks after the attacks, our boys were still living off of MREs and cold food trucked in from another FOB.

**IM – Jenn and James, January 2, 2005**

**Jenn: Did you get any food today?**

**James: Yeah, one meal**

Jenn: Was it more than bologna sandwiches?

James: Yes, only because we went to FOB Diamondback today

Jenn: What did you eat yesterday?

James: Bologna

Jenn: So sorry! How long will this go on?

James: Who knows, really

Jenn: Some parents are writing their senators about this food 'shortage'

James: Did you?

Jenn: I'm planning to call Sen. Lugar's office tomorrow if that's okay with you

James: Yes because we rarely go to Diamondback and I don't want that to be the only time we get decent food

Jenn: Well, I'll call his office first thing tomorrow and I'll call Sen. Evan Bayh too

James: OK, that's good

Jenn: Just so I have my facts straight when I start calling the senators can you tell me a couple more things about the food

James: OK

Jenn: Are they serving anything else besides cold cut sandwiches

James: Like MREs, not much else

Jenn: Have they told you when there will be regular meal service again?

James: NO

Jenn: I'm so sorry you can't get fed! Who is your commander?

James: Our BDE Commander is Colonel Brown

Jenn: I'm sure Colonel Brown is doing all he can. I'm going to fix you all the great big meals you want when you get home. Some pressure needs to be put on your food contractor

James: Yeah, it's KBR

Jenn: See, your mess hall probably had plenty of supplies - but many of those would have been destroyed and are unusable without a kitchen. Any food they would have had on order would be for a 'kitchen. So, now they've got to figure out how to feed you guys without the kitchen.

James: Yeah

Jenn: It's simply logistics - but you probably don't care how simple it is when you are hungry.

James: Yeah we don't

Jenn: You doing okay besides no food?

James: Yeah, I'm good

Jenn: I hate to log off, but I've got to go

James: OK

Jenn: Are you going to be around later you think?

James: Yeah I think so; the $82^{nd}$ is coming in today so we may have patrol

Jenn: Okay, well bye for now, and hopefully we can talk later

James: OK, I'll try to get online later

Jenn: I'm getting pissed about this food shortage! I'll let our senators know first thing tomorrow

James: I'm pissed too Jenn, believe me

Jenn: Well, take care and if I don't talk to you today, I'll write you and let you know how those phone calls go, okay? I mean, you joined the Army, not prison!

James: Thanks Jenn- you're good at bitching!

Jenn: That's funny!

James: I gotta go now

Jenn: Well, bye for now. Just hang in there - you're doing great! I am so proud of you - I love you pal!

James: I love you too Jenn

*IM – Patti and Jenn, February 22, 2005, eight weeks after the mess hall attack*

*Jenn: Do you know if the mess hall still closed?*

*Patti: YEP*

*Jenn: I could build it faster than that*

*Patti: It opened it for about 1 day, then they closed it because the bunkers were not finished that surround it.*

*Jenn: How ridiculous*

*Patti: I would like to know who has that particular contract. I would bet my teeth that snake Chaney is involved.*

*Jenn: Could be the company KBR - I wouldn't want to be one of the people that is making money off of this war.*

*Patti: There are plenty of them...*

*Jenn: It just doesn't seem like it should be this way...having to worry about kids fighting a war that NO ONE understands. I wasn't around during Vietnam, but I imagine the war moms then felt a lot like we do now.*

*Patti: Yes - but probably worse...they didn't have IM, They didn't have the majority of the public behind the troops*

*Jenn: Yeah, it's good to know how many people are supporting our troops despite the cause*

*Patti: Thanks, I really needed to vent. Bye for now*

*Jenn: You can vent with me anytime!! I love chatting with you – ttyl*

Not only was food scarce, but the Army seemed to have trouble even getting supplies for the troops. After the mess hall bombing, all the Iraqi employees were fired because security had been breached and no one escaped suspicion in the attack.  My brother had several pieces of clothing at the laundry, which closed for a time after the attack. The pair of pants that he was wearing the day of the mess hall attack were blood stained and needed to be thrown away, but since he had no other pair, this was not an option. James inquired about getting a new pants, and was told it would take 10-12 weeks.  I told my brother that we would try to find a pair here in the U.S. and send them over.

My father phoned a nearby Army supply store, and the owner not only found a pair in James' size but found appropriate insignia – all the next day. He shipped them to my father overnight, and they were promptly packed up and shipped to James in Iraq. I remember telling Patti this story in one of our online chats. We were both so extremely frustrated at the Army's inability to procure the most basic of supplies, such as food and clothing. If it was so hard to get decent food and pants, was the military also having trouble getting bullets and helmets?

*The families of our soldiers had tried hard to meet the postal shipping deadlines for Christmas deliveries to Iraq. We tried to the best of our abilities to send "Christmas in a Box". Cookies were baked, decorated and "shrink wrapped", to try to preserve them. Miniature Christmas trees with tiny decorations were purchased. Gag gifts and toys were sent to help pass the difficult time. Chocolates, which survive shipping in winter, were stuffed into little stockings with other candy for soldiers to share with platoon-mates. We shipped anything we could think of to try to soften the blow of a lonely Christmas at war.*

*The ripple effect of the mess tent explosion was far greater than we had imagined. Jenn and I were angered and puzzled that on Dec 25th our soldiers were eating cold bologna sandwiches. Though this upset us, we were so THANKFUL that they were alive.*

*During the Christmas holiday, Secretary of Defense Donald Rumsfeld made a surprise visit to Mosul, Iraq. Newspaper and television reports showed Mr. Rumsfeld visiting the wounded and eating breakfast with soldiers. We wondered during the aftermath of the mess hall attack and with a shortage of food on base, why couldn't the Secretary either have brought food stores with him to give to the soldiers or be served the same scant amount of food our soldiers were receiving? It seemed to us that the richest Army in the world was not able to provide adequate nutrition for our soldiers at FOB Marez.*

*As always, it took the Army time to figure out how to repair a "destroyed" supply chain. In this case, food for Deuce Four. During that time, our guys survived on MREs and food from the boxes the families had been sending. There was little more than one meal a day. And THEN, the second wave of the ripple affect hit. Mail delivery to our soldiers STOPPED. Later we learned the stoppage was due to the increased security on the FOB and, in rapid succession, the increasing security in Mosul, which was preparing for the upcoming election. This meant few deliveries were being transported into the area. Our frantically packed and expensively shipped care packages of food were stranded in Germany.*

*For the most part, our soldiers knew less than we did about what was causing the problem. They just knew that they were hungry, losing weight, and it seemed nobody cared.*

*Jon later told us,*

> **"After the mess hall was blown up there was mass confusion. We had upped a lot of our patrols... we all lost a lot of weight because now they had to truck our food in from another FOB. At first it was only dinner. But, after enough complaining, we got breakfast and dinner, or you could eat an MRE. Well, as any soldier will tell you if they have dined on MREs for any period of time, not only are they some of the worst meals you could ever eat, but they will also constipate you, really bad. I think it's something they do on purpose. So we were down to one meal a day because of the way the rotation of the patrols went. You either missed breakfast or you missed dinner. You were out on patrol or just getting back and you were so tired after that was done, that you just didn't want to go and eat. So,**

*we all were very upset, and very edgy on that. There*
*was a lot of fighting among our soldiers, thankfully no*
*one pulled any weapons on each other, but the fist*
*fights, things like that, did kick up a bit."*

*Jenn and I began contacting everybody we could dream up about*
*this situation. I wrote to all the Congressional representatives*
*and Senators in Arizona. Jenn did the same in Indiana. Largely,*
*this was a waste of time and postage. I will say, the ONLY office*
*to respond to me was Senator McCain's office. I could not say*
*McCain's office did anything more than call about 6 weeks after*
*I wrote. In Indiana, Jenn was contacted several times by Dick*
*Lugar's office regarding the matter.*

*We did finally get a little help from an unlikely source. My*
*brother Larry, in California, worked with a very sweet lady,*
*whose father was a General in the National Guard. The General*
*was in Kuwait at the time. This nice woman advised her father*
*of the situation. He was then able to give some attention to*
*improving the mail delivery to FOB Marez. Shortly after the*
*General's intervention, our guys started receiving mail again.*

*You may not think that is so important. After all, the Army will*
*take care of the soldiers' needs, right? Well, there's no doubt at*
*all about how important mail from home is when you read these*
*words from Jon when we asked if he liked receiving mail and*
*packages.*

**"I really didn't know anyone who didn't like getting**
**mail. It kind of let you know that your loved ones were**
**still thinking of you."**

*For the loved ones at home, sending care packages was the one thing that could be done for your soldier. For some of us, it was the activity that kept us centered and connected to reality. No matter what else went on, the box we had in progress was kept open in the kitchen. Every trip to the store or cleaning of a room involved deciding which things would be best to send in the next box. In the appendix, under packages, we have listed some of the things our soldiers seemed to like the best. But really, what was in the box was far less important that the knowledge that someone cared enough to pack and send it to them.*

# BEFORE IRAQ

My brother James joined the military just days after 9-11. He signed at age 17, while still in high school as part of the Army's delayed entry plan. Since he had taken all the classes that he needed to graduate from high school, he decided to leave high school early and start boot camp.

The only part of high school that ever interested my brother was football. Football was the one thing that kept my brother focused and out of trouble. We jokingly called him "Rudy" because he never missed a practice, a run, a footage film, a conditioning – NEVER. Even though our own family had fallen apart, James' football family was always there for him.

Football season ended in November, and he could see no other reason to prolong the start of his Army contract. In March 2002, my brother left rural Indiana for Ft. Benning, Georgia. There is no good time to start basic training at Ft. Benning. The winter nights are freezing cold, and the summer days are stiflingly humid.

Ft. Benning is in the heart of Georgia and is the home of the infantry. It is here that the Army trains all types of infantry soldiers, from mechanized to airborne rangers and everything in between. The base is enormous, covering over 180,000 unforgiving acres. In the heart of the base is Sand Hill, home of infantry basic training. There's an old

World War I era military song that sums up Ft. Benning, *"My home is old Ft. Benning, the land that God forgot."*

Sand Hill is a mountain deep in the woods of Ft. Benning. In order for infantry soldiers to graduate and receive their signature blue infantry cord, they must low-crawl climb to the top of the mountain. It's a right of passage that isn't easily earned. Ft. Benning is where soldiers learn to survive and to kill. Period. Only the strong survive; the weak are slowly and painfully weeded out, sent back home or moved to less demanding training facilities. The surface is bare sand - all the vegetation has been worn away over the decades. The hill itself is covered with wire, broken glass and booby traps. Those that make it to the top earn the right to call themselves U.S. Army Infantrymen.

I cried the day my brother left for basic training. I was convinced that he would never survive the grueling physical and emotional tests the drill sergeants would put him through. Our family is a 'can't family'. We grew up hearing the words "I can't, you can't, we can't, it can't be done" everyday. Of course, I was wrong. I'm glad now that he was pushed so hard. Basic training is tough for a reason – so that the troops can be prepared for combat.

It is funny now to think about how worried I was during basic training. After all, it's just training. The real worries come when our soldiers are placed in battle in a real war.

The one place my soldier and many others found peace and strength during basic training was in church.

Harmony Church at Ft. Benning is packed every service. During family weekend I visited the base and tagged along for Sunday services. The church was packed. Not only were there not enough seats for the soldiers, there wasn't enough standing room for the soldiers either. Many stood outside the front door leaning on each other as they listened in. When we arrived, soldiers left the pew so that we could be seated. It was one of the most beautiful, moving church services I have ever attended.

During the service, every mouth opened to sing and every head bowed for prayers. Without orders, each soldier in the church was succinct. Many of the soldiers had their field bibles with them, already worn a bit from reading. During the service, the chaplain asked for prayer requests. For nearly 30 minutes, soldiers stood one by one asking for prayers to support those left back home. One soldier's wife was nine months pregnant with twins, another's grandmother had just passed away. Each request was so unselfish that I was moved to tears. These men would soon be fighting in the war on terror, but their primary concern was for the safety and happiness of their loved ones back home.

What the chaplains at Ft. Benning and other basic training bases know is that they must nurture the living while they can, because on the battlefield they must also care for the wounded, and then honor the dead. I think all Americans should adopt this motto when it comes to our soldiers and veterans.

My brother graduated from the Infantry at Ft. Benning, Georgia on July 3rd. It was a moving, emotional graduation for many reasons. Anytime a soldier graduates from training and begins his military career, there is a wide spectrum of mixed emotions. When a soldier does so during wartime, those emotions are magnified a million fold. In addition to graduation being held during wartime, it was also adjacent to the first celebration of our nation's birth since the 9-11 attacks. Many of the soldiers in the Ft. Benning graduation ceremony that day were from the New York City area. You see, after 9-11, many Americans, especially New Yorkers, felt such an obligation to country that they joined the military hoping to "fight the good fight" and avenge the deaths of 9-11. Just as our country had gone guns blazing into Iraq and Afghanistan, the new Infantry soldiers were ready to join the fight.

I wasn't ready. There is no basic training for family members. Support groups exist and they are great, but nothing can be done to prepare you for the deployment of your loved one.

---

*When Jon was in Iraq, in 2004 and 2005, friends and family would ask me, "How did you ever LET this happen? Why did you LET him join?"*

*This may seem like a reasonable question, but to a loved one it cuts like a knife. The questions are too close to the quick, and bring to air the secret questions of the heart that I asked myself in sleepless hours of worry. Now, having had years to heal, I can look back on these questions and try to honestly sort through and answer them.*

*Our son Jon is a wonderful person. From boyhood, he was sweet and gentle, while tall and handsome. He was NOT a Rhodes Scholar. In some ways, Jon had to work hard to reach normal growth scales; in many other ways, he was gifted. But, in short, he never conformed.*

*He went to high school and graduated on time, but there was doubt about that right up to three days before graduation. Jon went to community college for one year and did OK. At the end of the summer of 2001, Jon left home, leaving a note for his devastated mother, that he thought it was better if he left and made his own life. With a ¾ painted house that Jon and I had been working on together, and my husband Tom coming home in a few days, I cried, went to work, and painted in the evening, to get over the hurt.*

*Jon found himself a job and moved into a tiny little trailer with his girlfriend, and tried to make a life for himself. For about two years he struggled with this, having several jobs, discovering the girlfriend was really no friend at all, and generally living in terrible conditions. For the most part, we were out of his life, except for an occasional visit. Tom and I did not like this and worked hard to maintain some communications for the day we knew would come when Jon decided to return home for help.*

*That day came in the winter of 2002. Jon returned for a tentative visit with his dad, describing his situation and after a few days of discussion he decided to move back home until he could find a job and get on his feet again.*

*One of Jon's brothers, Tommy, was working for a Heating and Air Conditioning company and got Jon a job. Not surprisingly, Jon was in this job a few months, and when the economy took a downturn, the boss had to reduce headcount, and Jon was out of work again.*

*We talked to Jon about returning to school, but he really didn't want any part of that. And, finally, Jon and his dad went to visit the recruiters. Tom tried to influence Jon to only accept an MOS that would assure a non-combat assignment, but, in the end, Jon was 22 years-old and made his own decision to enlist with an MOS of 91W, commonly known as Combat Medic. This was approximately February of 2003. Jon received no signing bonus. He just wanted to get a trade and a new start on life.*

*To put these decisions in context, the Iraq WAR had not started...President Bush was warning of danger and weapons of mass destruction, but there was no evidence. Tom and I could NOT believe the U.S.A. would invade Iraq without solid evidence. Surely, NO thinking president would engage in such a war. Of course, we were very wrong.*

*When President Bush announced the invasion of Iraq on March 20, 2003, we were shocked and appalled. Our son would leave for boot camp May 20, 2003. We had no choice at that point but to encourage our son and pray the senseless conflict would be over by the time he finished training. He had nine weeks of Basic*

*Training and 16 weeks of AIT to become a medic…surely it would be over by then, we hoped.*

*On the 19th of May, Jon left for Phoenix, was sworn into the Army, and was flown to Ft. Sill, Oklahoma, for basic training. We knew we would not hear from him much during the first four weeks of basic training. Jon sent the required letters inspired by his sergeant. You can read Jon's letter from basic training in the Appendix.*

*In early June, Tom left for our cottage in Canada, and stayed there working on what we hope will one day be our retirement cottage. I stayed in Arizona with our son Tommy, who was working and going to college. To be honest, I was relieved since I knew Jon would be carefully watched, live in relative cleanliness, and have regular food and exercise. After the previous years, it was a blessing.*

*That summer my work required me to travel a lot, including two trips to Taiwan and several other business trips. I was able to arrange a trip to Oklahoma in conjunction with another business trip to see Jon graduate from Basic Training. It was July and very, very hot and humid. I must say, the graduation exercises, discipline displayed, and my son's genuine happiness that I was there warmed my heart. The sergeants even let the recruits stay overnight off base with their families for one night. That night, Jon and I went to The Outback Steakhouse for steak and birthday cake – since he had just had his 22nd birthday on June 22nd.*

*It was funny. I had made reservations at a hotel - sight unseen - and oh my goodness what a rattrap that place was. The next morning I checked out and moved to a nicer hotel. It was such a pleasure seeing my tired but proud Jon, resting and relaxing in that hotel room.*

*The day after graduation, Jon and a few others going to 91W training flew from a small airport in Oklahoma to Dallas and then to San Antonio. They were headed for Ft. Sam Houston and 16 weeks of AIT training. It was a bittersweet time. One of the soldiers in HQ gave me a tip that no one could stop me from going to the airport and waiting with the soldiers. He also told me the approximate time they would be at the airport would be 4 AM. So I bought donuts the night before, got up early, and went to see them off. They were all pretty nervous and not many of the donuts were eaten, but I got to be with Jon for an additional four hours, and was able to meet a couple of his friends. I took photos to share with my husband when I got home. I also took some photos of a fellow who was very young, 20 I think, who had a wife and two children at home. The young family could not afford to travel to be with him. I printed and sent photos with a little letter by mail to that young woman, but I never heard anything more of them. It struck me that this "no other choice" selection of the Armed Forces as a career was repeated again and again as I met Jon's friends, our country's soldiers.*

*Jon was in AIT until near Thanksgiving time, in 2003. We did hear from Jon by phone fairly frequently while he was at Ft. Sam Houston. He did OK most of the time in his testing...a few times he was close to washing out I think, but the Army makes sure they get a proper percentage of soldiers who pass by cramming information into them and then retesting until they pass. I think a proper mix of the Army training methods with public school system methods might be a big improvement.*

*Jon met a cute little girl in San Antonio. I think she was hoping to become part of his family, but later it became clear she was a passing fancy. Jon, since manhood, has been popular with the ladies. And, he is strikingly handsome, so it is no wonder!*

*Jon told us of a field training exercise where a "soldier" was at the bottom of a ravine and had to be transported to a suitable helicopter landing site. He did very well in that exercise and was able to haul the "wounded" soldier up a very steep grade and got him to the pick up point as required. His "wounded" soldier was delivered "alive" to the helicopter team.*

*Tom returned to Arizona in August. We had decided earlier in the summer to attend his graduation from AIT together. We had never been to San Antonio and thought it would be pleasant, and it was an important occasion.*

*We were there several days. Tom's buddy from high school who lives in Houston drove to San Antonio to celebrate with us. We were able to have Jon with us for a couple of nights of walking the Riverwalk and eating nice dinners. We visited the tiny Alamo historical site. We took Jon and his date to the zoo. It was a lovely time and we were very proud of our son's accomplishment.*

*On graduation day, as I saw the sea of young faces, happy but pensive, and listened to the Army officers speak, I began to focus on an obvious fact. There were young women, very small men,*

*many, many types of soldiers in the 91W graduating class...and
Jon and a very few others towered over the group. At 6 ft 4 in,
200 lb, strong and good looking and of strong stock...there was
NO CHANCE that he would not be assigned to an infantry
unit. My son would be a Soldier Medic in a dangerous war zone
very soon. I had awakened from my denial stage with a start and
a few quickly hidden tears.*

*Jon left the following day, headed for Ft. Lewis, Washington. He
joined his unit there, Deuce Four, A-Company, and started
learning his duties. He would not come home until Christmas.
He wanted to save his leave for the holidays. We thought it
might be our last Christmas together for a long while, though we
didn't know for certain. As it turns out, we were correct. Due to
circumstance, some good, some bad, Jon has not been home for
Christmas on Dec 25<sup>th</sup> since that year.*

*It had been seven months since Jon had been home when he
returned to Arizona for Christmas in December of 2003.. He had
completed Basic training at Ft. Sill, Oklahoma, had immediately
gone to Ft. Sam Houston for 91W training, and had then been
attached to Deuce Four's A-Company at Ft. Lewis in
Washington State. He was anxious to have some time with his
brothers. Jon's Grandma decided to join us for Christmas, too.
We all knew that this would be a memorable last Christmas
together for a while. We were right about the memorable part,
but as so often is the case in life, we had no idea what the reasons
for that would be.*

*We celebrated Christmas Eve, with lots of food, young folks
singing Karaoke, and general holiday festivities. We went to*

*church and much of our congregation visited with Jon and wished him well.*

*After Grandma and Jon arrived, we decided that it would be fun to make a trip to the Yuma Sand Dunes. This had been a tradition for us as the boys were growing up. Every year, the day after Christmas, we would roll in our motor home, with a trailer of sand rails and ATVs behind. A couple of the boys' current girlfriends came along. Even Grandma was excited about her first trip to the dunes.*

*Just before the trip, Grandma became ill. We attributed her illness to travel and assumed she would feel better after settling in. We took Grandma to the doctor, got some antibiotics, and carried on with our celebrations.*

*The day after Christmas, we loaded up Grandma, and all our stuff, and headed for the dunes. We had a tire blowout on the trip that required an unscheduled "limping" trip to a small town along the way, but we got a new tire and continued. This is a pretty small event for the rugged Donahue Gang. We arrived at the dunes and settled in for the night. Unfortunately, Grandma was still not feeling any better, but was having fun nonetheless.*

*The sand dunes are located between Yuma, Arizona and Blythe, California. They are very near the border of Mexico, at the southern convergence of the Mexican border and the state line of Arizona and California. There are miles, and miles of soft, fine, hourglass, white sand in a series of rolling hills. During the winter holidays, thousands of people haul their sand vehicles into the desert and these eerie and oddly beautiful dunes become an adult sandbox full of motorized "toys". Otherwise sober men become "devils on wheels". Days are filled with zooming around the lip of a sand bowl, just barely missing a witches eye at the bottom, racing to the top of a steep and long hill of sand, only to turn around and gaze at the valley far below, and then drop the nose of the vehicle back over the top of the hill to fly back down to the bottom. It is wildly exciting, especially for the those experiencing it for the first time.*

*Even though Grandma was having fun, she was still sick. We phoned our family doctor who advised us to get Grandma to a hospital as soon as possible.*

*With only a little discussion, we loaded up the gear and headed to University Hospital in Tucson. Thankfully,Grandma's condition improved after just a few days.*

*Our final Christmas visit with Jon was mixed with concern for Grandma, travel to the sand dunes, visits to the hospital, as well as managing our jobs and the usual tasks of every day life. Looking back I can see it was all a blessing because none of us had any spare time to indulge in worry about Jon's probable deployment to a war zone.*

# THE PRICE OF WAR

The price of war is immeasurable and always too high.

On January 25, 2005, at 13:54 local time, James ran over an IED while driving his Stryker vehicle. It was 05:54 back home in Indiana, and I started my day just like any other Tuesday during the deployment. I logged on to my computer, checked email, and found no messages from Iraq. After getting my son off to school, I headed to town to run errands. My cell phone rang and I did not recognize the number on the caller id, so I almost did not answer. Because I hoped it was my brother calling from a pay phone on the FOB to say hello, I decided to pick up.

When I first answered my phone, I couldn't hear anything on the other end of the line. Then I heard a man's voice that I didn't recognize ask if I was James' sister. I could barely respond a simple 'yes' because my throat was swelling up and tears were filling my eyes. My heart raced. Surely, I would not be notified that James was killed over the phone.

Then I heard the dear sound of my little brother on the other end of the phone. He had been driving his Stryker through a neighborhood while the rest of his squad was on a raid when he ran over an IED. The explosion crippled the vehicle and slammed James and another soldier inside around like pinballs. James was phoning me from the

101

combat field hospital from his commander's satellite phone, which is why I did not recognize the phone number on my caller id.

James and the other soldier had concussions, but were otherwise unharmed. The treatment at the time for James' concussion was little more than a day off work and some Tylenol. We did not know until much later the true damage caused to his brain that day.

"Hey Jenn, it's me James, are you there?"

"Yes, I'm here. James, where are you? Are you okay?"

"Jenn, I ran over some garbage that exploded."

"What? When? Are you hurt?"

"It was earlier today, a few hours ago. I'm at the hospital and they are going to do some tests on my head. I have a concussion and my ears are ringing real bad."

"So other than your head, you are okay? You weren't hit by shrapnel? You don't have any broken bones?"

"No, just my head. It hurts bad and I can't hear anything out of my right ear. I'm dizzy right now, but the doctor said that will go away after I get some rest."

"Was anyone else with you? Is anyone else wounded?"

"It was just me and another guy in the Stryker, Roberto. He's going to be okay, too."

"Oh thank God! You are so lucky. James, I love you and I wish I could be there for you."

"It's okay Jenn, I'm tough. Just like you always said, I've got a really hard head."

That was my little brother. Making jokes during the darkest of times.

"Are you on a pay phone? How are you able to call me?"

"Well, the battalion has this satellite phone and they let me use it so I could call you and tell you I was hurt before you heard it from somebody else."

"I'm so glad you called. If I read about this in the chat rooms I think my heart would stop. What are they going to do now? Will you stay in the hospital? Do you have to go back to duty?"

"I am going to stay in here for awhile until they get all my tests back, then I guess I'll go back to my company. I really dunno."

As we spoke, my thoughts raced. I can remember feeling sick to my stomach as we spoke. When the conversation ended, I was completely overcome with emotions. I phoned my husband, father and friends so that we could pray. That day we prayed prayers of thanksgiving and for healing.

James was driving his Stryker around the neighborhood while the rest of his squad was conducting a raid. As he and Roberto, the other crew member drove slowly around the block, patrolling and waiting for his squad to return, he ran over some garbage that contained an IED. Stryker vehicles are tough. Fortunately, James was protected from the blast and shrapnel. Two of the 19-ton vehicle's eight wheels were completely blown off. The blast left a hole in the ground, but the steel grill that surrounds the outside of the Stryker vehicle body provided adequate protection from any debris that might have ripped apart a Humvee in a similar attack.

James was found unconscious by his squad, who rushed to the vehicle when they heard the blast. They brought him to with smelling salts and immediately took him and Roberto to the combat support hospital. No civilians were injured. The streets had emptied just before the blast. Of course, no one responsible for the bomb was apprehended, at least not because of that offense. It was a nameless, faceless attack, like so many others in this war.

At the hospital in Iraq James received a CAT scan, which showed no signs of brain damage at the time, and was given earplugs before being returned to duty. With the elections looming in just days, no platoon could be short a man, especially not a driver.

In the weeks that followed the blast that injured my brother, I researched concussions and did my best to follow the state of his health. I worried that, in a weakened state, he would make a mistake and be wounded again, or worse. I had less contact with him during his recovery time that I wanted. I understand that when your head is pounding and you don't feel well the last thing you probably want to do is stand in line for two hours so that you can use the computer for who knows how long just to talk to your sister who worries too much. When I did have the chance to chat with James, I asked about his health and tried as best I could from so far away to offer him comfort.

IM – Jenn and James, February 20, 2005

Jenn: Did you eat today?

James: Yeah, I'm still eating that big box of food the church sent

Jenn: How's your ear?

James: It's still ringing

Jenn: I hope that stops soon - I know it's driving you crazy

James: It might be permanent

Jenn: We'll take you to see some specialists when you get home

James: I think I can see a specialist when I get back to Fort Lewis

Jenn: Well if they don't fix it at Lewis then we'll go anywhere we need to -there are lots of VA hospitals

James: Do you think the VA has good doctors?

**Jenn: We'll find one with the best, I'll make some calls & find out where they have the hearing specialists.**

My brother struggled with hearing impairment, headaches, and mood swings for the remainder of the deployment. Still today, James suffers from disabling side effects, including seizures, because of his Traumatic Brain Injury, or TBI, from the blast and the PTSD that plagues him.

Many of the symptoms for TBI and PTSD are the same. This has made treatment difficult. Fortunately, he lives just an hour from the VA hospital and makes weekly visits for treatment. It is estimated that 20 percent or more of combat troops returning from the wars in Iraq and Afghanistan will suffer from TBI and as many as 50 percent will suffer from PTSD. As of December 2008, that number could be 300,000 veterans or more. These unseen injuries are just one price of war that our country will pay for generations.

Because little research has been done on the long-term effects war-related concussions have on the brain, much of the treatment my brother receives is trial and error. He has literally been on dozens of medications, and receives counseling as part of his injury complications. With daily life constantly interrupted by the complaints brought on by his brain injury, including seizures, headaches, hearing impairment, insomnia, nightmares, memory loss, confusion, and more, transitioning back into civilian life has been a challenge.

For other soldiers, the price of war paid was even higher than that of my brother. On February 19, 2005, one special soldier paid the ultimate price.

Despite having been wounded in the mess hall attack, Clint Gertson persevered, helping others more seriously wounded and then returning to his duty as a first rate sniper. When communication with our soldiers ceased for several days in mid-February, we knew someone had been killed, but did not know who. We waited, anxiously as we selfishly hoped it would not be our soldier. After the standard blackout following a soldier's death, our boys were able to reach out to us. Knowing that your loved one wasn't the soldier killed or wounded is comforting, but also makes you feel incredibly selfish because you know another family is feeling indescribable pain.

**IM – Jenn and James, February 20, 2005**

**James: Hey Jenn**

**Jenn: Hey –can you talk for a while?**

**James: Not for long, I'll be on later though**

**Jenn: Okay, CNN just showed a bunch of you guys in Mosul watching the Daytona 500, that was neat**

**\*\*long pause, no response from James but I can see that he is still logged into IM\*\***

**Jenn: Everything okay?**

**James: NO**

Jenn: What's wrong?

James: It sucks when your friend dies

Jenn: What was his name? I will pray for his family

James: Clint Gertson. I guess I'm getting another memorial bracelet

**James wears remembrance bracelets for his friends killed in Mosul**

Jenn: My heart hurts for you right now

James: Yeah…it was a drive by

Jenn: Bastards! Will you find who did it?

James: NO

Jenn: There isn't anything I can say to make you feel better, but I'm praying.

James: I know – thanks for that. Clint was from Texas

Jenn: Did he have kids?

James: He was single, with no kids

Jenn: I'm sorry for his parents & for you guys - you're just like family over there

James: Yeah we are family

James: It was CPT Van's fault

Jenn: No, it's the terrorists' fault, you are in a bad situation you can't control

James: Well there were like 7 guys just standing around each other

Jenn: Is that what you are supposed to do?

James: No, we should have been spread out

Jenn: Well, mistakes happen. The one to blame is the person pulling the trigger

James: Yeah, I guess

Jenn: Being mad at the Captain won't bring your friend back

James: I know...I agree

Jenn: You gonna be able to get some sleep tonight?

James: Yeah I think so

Jenn: Just remember that your friend is in heaven now, even though he didn't deserve death, he's getting richly rewarded

James: I know. I have to go but I'll talk to you guys later...I love you guys


IM- Jenn and James, February 21, 2005

Jenn: Your friend Clint's death was on the news this morning

James: Yeah

Jenn: I'm real sorry for his family. I've been praying for them all day

James: Yeah...it's hard

Jenn: You guys must be going through a lot

James: You have no idea

Jenn: Is there anything at all that I can do to help? The things I'm doing here seem so unimportant right now.

James: Could you send some flowers to the funeral?

Jenn: It will be my honor.

James: Thanks...goodnight Jenn

*IM – Patti and Jenn, February 22, 2005*

*Patti: Sorry to bother you...I see you are online with James...how is he?*

*Jenn: They had a big memorial service for Clint*

*Patti: OH MAN - that is rough, but necessary for their grieving process.*

*Jenn: Since James is online right now, I'll ask about how Jon is doing*

*\*\*We pause our conversation so that I can check in quickly with James\*\**

*Jenn: Just heard back, James had to go - he said Jon was doing okay*

*Patti: Thank you. I feel so bad that our guys are going through these terrible disappointments*

*Jenn: James said they just feel like robots - not knowing what they are going to do day to day*

*Jenn: I'd like to see President Bush go a year plus without seeing his kids*

*Patti: Worse than that, what if his daughters were fighting in Mosul? Let's propose a constitutional amendment...Presidents cannot declare war unless their own kids are in the military!*

*Jenn: Have you seen the movie Fahrenheit 9-11*

*Patti: YES*

*Jenn: Amazing how few congressmen have kids in the military, but so easy for them to vote to send our kids to war*

*Patti: The congressmen and senators with the Marines brochure...great scene. How dare they vote to put our kids in danger!*

It was infuriating how common, everyday Americans were worrying every minute at home about their soldiers in harms way. When Clint Gertson died, another part of our soldiers, and of us died, too. Good, decent soldiers with a lifetime ahead of them were being needlessly sacrificed for a cause that was not justified. Clint represented all that was wrong with this war: innocence lost, goodness stolen by evil, right losing to wrong. As much as it hurt to talk about it, Jon had some wonderful reflections of Clint.

*"Clint Gertson was a big, tall happy go lucky guy. You always saw him with a chew in his mouth and a smile on his face. He was one of these guys that if you asked him for anything…he would just find a way to get it done for you. The first time I really met him, we were about 4 days away from deployment and I had driven my car down to Oregon, which, of course, I wasn't supposed to do…I was supposed to stay within 50 miles of the base. On the way back, the engine had blown . Almost everyone had already put their vehicles in storage, but Clint still had his truck because he was helping someone move. So I said to Clint, 'Hey, my car is down in Oregon , I need some help, is there any way I could, you know, persuade you into helping me out?' He didn't say, 'Well, let me check,' or, 'I have things to do.' Without any hesitation, Clint said, 'Hey, not a problem.' He drove all the way straight down to Oregon and we brought my car right back. He actually called up his family and said, 'Hey, I can't come over and help you move today, I got to go help one of the guys in my platoon out.' That was the type of guy he was. He would just drop everything to help his own soldiers. He was a guy that was someone you could look up to. We did give him a little bit of static sometimes. Clint was one of the snipers for AlphA-Company. He missed a shot once, but it was only about 100 meters away. It was a guy with a mortar tube.*

*Then Clint fired a second time and we weren't sure if he hit the guy or not, but the guy dropped the mortar tube so I guess the end result was that Clint got the mortar tube away from the enemy. We kind of demanded a one shot, one kill type thing from the snipers, so that's why we gave him some static. Anyways, Clint was one of the guys that we all loved. You wouldn't find anyone in that company that disliked him."*

Clint Gertson was dearly loved by all. In the opinion of the soldiers, his death illustrated the change in leadership and reminded them of the security they lost when Captain J was killed. Clint was a brother. Despite of and because of losing him, our soldiers had to go on.

# SETTLING IN

Like everything in life, as the deployment carried on, so did we. Soon our routines began to develop. We learned that when chatting online with our soldiers to expect they will log off unexpectedly. We learned that seeing our guys online meant we could stop holding our breath, at least for the few moments while we were chatting. Their missions were dangerous, but creative and well planned. The more terrorists they captured or killed, the fewer the attacks and that kept them motivated.

**IM – Jenn and James, March 1, 2005**

**Jenn: The terrorists keep releasing videos of their attacks in Mosul - isn't that ridiculous? I think you should start looking for people with video cameras in odd places**

**James: Actually, we do. They tried to tape us yesterday while they were shooting at us. That was a big mistake**

**Jenn: B@#%ds!**

**James: We got 'em though!**

**Jenn: Good!**

Back home, as we muddled through our daily lives, Deuce Four was fully engaged in combat operations. We were glad that our guys were capturing terrorists and really putting down the insurgency. Many times our soldiers would capture or kill terrorists and find they had been using video cameras to not only preserve a memory of their attacks, but to learn from them and improve their operations. Cell phones and radios captured during raids were an enormous benefit. Not only did their confiscation keep a detonator out of the insurgents' hands, but cell phone records provided valuable information such as enemy location and civilian cooperation.

The battalion was so aggressive in the battle for Mosul that several reporters and photographers were embedded with our soldiers. A team from the Associated Press seemed to have photographs published nearly every day in print or on television. Sometimes I would see the photos in our hometown newspaper. Other times, I would see them on the cover of *The New York Times* or *USA Today* at the newsstand in the grocery. We followed a journalist named Michael Yon who provided gritty, honest reports.

In the early part of the deployment, the pictures were ominous. Often the photos would show Deuce Four soldiers searching for insurgents, raiding a home or warehouse, or on patrol. The glimpses into the lives of our loved ones at war were both depressing and exhilarating. They made me feel so conflicted; proud and yet unimportant – close but yet so very far away. Our soldiers were also feeling conflicted from the thrill of battle when they put down insurgents and then the agony of defeat when they lost one of their own.

On March 31, 2005, *The Washington Post* published an article questioning the safety and readiness of the Stryker vehicle for combat. I had always felt some comfort knowing that James, as a driver, might be better protected inside the Stryker than in a Humvee. He often stayed inside the vehicle while the rest of his squad would exit and conduct raids in the street or inside Iraqi homes. When James drove his Stryker over the IED, I realized that although he was safer in a Stryker than in a Humvee, he was still at great risk, all the time. And there was nothing I could do to minimize that risk. The *Post's* article brought to light several flaws in the Stryker that I worried would impact the protection it offered my brother as a driver.

While we had our routines of assembling and shipping care packages, checking our email and instant message accounts, and phoning each other to check in, we could never adjust to the stress of constant danger. The danger of injury or death for our soldiers was endless.

Every soldier handles the pressure of deployment differently. At first, my brother James relieved his stress by joking around a lot.

*"At first," Jon told us, "James was very fun to get along with. But, as we got more and more desensitized to the explosions and the shootings and things like that, it changed him... I think it was just the pressure of being away and being on a deployment like that, and actually being shot at. Putting yourself in a place*

*where overall everyone hates you there. That really changed everyone."*

Other soldiers became introverted, which to an outsider would appear as laziness. In reality, some of the soldiers who spent time alone, writing letters home and studying their faith handled the stress surprisingly well. There is no way to say who handled the stress the best during the deployment. Whether it was the soldier who lashed out at his family on the phone or internet, or the soldier who kept his feeling inside and spent time praying and meditating. Every soldier handles the stresses of war in different ways. Many soldiers sought the chaplain or medic for comfort and solace when times got tough. From counseling soldiers with financial trouble to comforting those with love affairs gone bad, there were always soldiers needing comfort from their brethren. But counseling was not Jon's primary job as a medic. He was there to provide immediate treatment for the wounded soldiers and even civilians. Sometimes it was just a quick bandage and then back to work. Other times, Jon was overwhelmed with need. We asked Jon how many people did he give medical attention to, and this is what he said.

*"I really cannot remember. Every day I would take temperatures, check their feet for new blisters, any new rashes, things like that for my own guys. I was basically like the platoon mom. Serious medical attention, I really couldn't tell you. If I gave a rough estimate, in the year that I was there, I would say probably 100 to 150. The majority of which was either*

*the ING, which is the Iraqi National Guard, or the Iraqi police,or it was just the regular population that would get hit in the cross fire. Most all the time, that's what it was. There was an IED or something like that would blow up in the neighborhood and absolutely no one had body armor on at all and they would just get shredded by this stuff. The worst one I got was when I was the only medic on scene for about 45 minutes. There were over 120 casualties from a roadside bomb in a real crowded area. The bomb was sitting in a car by the new ING recruits who were lining up. We were just following behind them and then this car blew up. It probably was supposed to go somewhere else but they found a target of opportunity and just blew them up. It was bad. I remember one girl that died, and it was really upsetting to me because she was hit in the chest and it had punctured her lung cavity. My guys found her. At first they didn't know it was serious. They didn't tell me about it until she had already had tracheal deviation, where her throat kind of pulled to the side, it's as your lungs are collapsing and filling full of blood. By the time that had happened, I mean, unless you're on an operating table with a very experienced surgeon standing over you, there is no way you are gonna make it."*

Scenes like that were a frequent and tragic occurrence. Besides tending to the needs of their own, our soldiers were faced with the aftermath of catastrophe inflicted on the defenseless. At home, we often felt moments of terror.

Terrified that our soldiers would be badly wounded or killed. Those feelings, however, pale in comparison to the type of terror our soldiers were feeling. We asked Jon about his scariest moment in Iraq.

*"The scariest moment I had was one of the days I was up pulling air guard out of the hatch inside the Stryker. I was looking down an alley and I remember there was a blue car, think it was an Opel. It drove by and I saw the barrel of an AK coming out and it started shooting and it fired 3 rounds. The $2^{nd}$ of the 3 hit a chem- light that was about a foot away from my face and I dropped down inside the Stryker because my face had this hot liquid on it and I was of course a little scared cause I thought...Oh God...I might have been hit cause, you know, it burned my eyes. And, then I figured out it was not me, it was a chem.-light that had gotten hit. It was a little too close for me."*

On the battlefield, our soldiers fought as one and tried to be as professional as possible. Just as the wives, sisters and mothers were working together at home to support each other, our soldiers were doing exactly the same in Iraq. No matter what, we were all there for each other. Jon told us about the people they were fighting, and how disjointed they were compared to our soldiers.

*"...the best way I could describe it is a lot like the gang elements that we have in our cities today. It was like a*

119

*bunch of young punks would grab an AK to shoot at us because it was a cool thing to do. But, the first second you came and confronted them, they wouldn't stand up with their belief. They would point a finger, point somewhere else. It was a very cowardly thing to do and it was very frustrating to us."*

*For all of us involved with the deployment, frustration was the cornerstone of the structure of our lives at that time. Usually the words "settling in" would imply some sort of comfortable time. I would hardly say there was ever a comfortable time during deployment. However, in the sense that routines were established, we had fewer moments of sheer panic, the tears decreased to occasional breakdowns instead of the instant eruptions in reaction to a simple, "How are you?" question from a neighbor...and we did settle in.*

# ELECTIONS

**Soldiers die so we can vote.**
**You dishonor them when you don't!**

I have never missed voting in an election. For me, this constitutional right is very important. I felt it was just as, if not more, important for my brother James to exercise his right to vote while he was in combat. Prior to deploying, I had the local election office send my brother an absentee ballot so that he could vote. He was intent on not missing his first chance to vote in the Presidential election.

**IM- Jenn and James November 3, 2004 (just a few days after Deuce Four arrived in Iraq, and it was the day after election day in the U.S.)**

**James: Hey Jenn, what time is it there?**

**Jenn: It's 10:10am and I was just thinking about you...
I stayed up until 4 am last night watching election coverage**

**James: I watched it this morning, too**

**Jenn: I think Bush is going to be the winner**

**James: Bush won, Ohio right?**

**Jenn: They haven't declared Ohio yet, still about 150,000 votes to count**

121

Jenn: Bush is leading there by 120,000 votes, so it's technically possible for Kerry to win Ohio still, but highly unlikely

Jenn: more people voted for bush in this election than any other president ever

James: Indiana voted for Bush right?

Jenn: Yeah, Indiana was like 70% for Bush & we were the first state to declare

James: my vote for Bush counted then

In the days before the elections in Iraq, which took place less than 90 days after the Presidential election in the U.S., my brother had significant changes in his attitude and state of mind. Most of these changes were due to his injury and returning to duty so quickly after the IED. It was at this point in the war that James became cold and callous.

IM with James January 27, 2005 (two days after James is wounded, three days before the Iraqi elections)

Jenn: Have you gone back to work

James: Yeah, how's that for ya? We went out today... I mean the elections are only in three days, so we really can't have guys out

Jenn: I think it's going to be bad during the election

James: I don't care, not my problem

Jenn: As long as you are okay

James: Yeah I'm better I guess

Jenn: Remember to eat and get plenty of water, that will help you recover more quickly

James: I'm trying... I found out we aren't getting mail until Feb. 2$^{nd}$

Jenn: Wow, that's next week...I guess that's for the best...I had an IM chat with your high school girlfriend today

James: Oh, is that right?

Jenn: She was glad to hear that you weren't more seriously injured - we all were

James: Yeah, well what's up with her? I don't even hear from her one time until I almost die-- what's up with that?

Jenn: I talked to her about that... she has found it difficult to find things to talk about...she didn't think you liked it when she asked you questions like 'what are you doing, what's it like there', she felt that talking about her everyday life was boring for you...I told her that's probably the kind of stuff you do want to hear about..normal everyday stuff from home might take your mind off of Iraq...it is hard for most people to find things to about with any soldier in Iraq ... do you understand?

James: Yeah, I guess

Jenn: What do you want to talk about or hear about? If you tell me that might help

James: Like how's people are doing & stuff going on in their life...cause I don't know being over here, I don't know anything

Jenn: Okay...what about from me, what kind of stuff should we be talking about?

James: I don't care

Jenn: Well, here's the stuff I'm doing today: dropping off Grandma's laundry, taking a bag of junk to goodwill, mailing some packages, taking the dog for a walk and cleaning the house

James: Yeah sounds fun...I miss Dixie (the dog)...I can't wait to see her

Jenn: Dixie will be so happy to see you, too

James: I bet

Jenn: How is your hearing today

James: The same

Jenn: Is your vision okay

James: A little blurry but not bad

Jenn: That should get better soon

James: Yeah, you think it will? Concussions suck

Jenn: Poor thing

James: I'll be fine I'm tough, right?

Jenn: Yes you are!!! I hope you can get some rest tonight

James: Nope – I won't – we have to work tonight

Jenn: Were you nervous going back to duty?

James: No not really

Jenn: That's good

James: Yeah, I'm tough

Jenn: It's probably normal to be a bit shaky after something like that

James: Yeah, but I'm tough remember?

Jenn: I know, but you ran over a FREAKING bomb

James: No, it went off next to me

Jenn:  Same thing

Jenn: Too bad you couldn't stay at the hospital longer to recuperate …remember, don't drink too much caffeine, okay, that's not good for your brain right now…even though you are tough

James: Yeah, i know

Jenn: Jon's mom sent me an email - she's real nice, she wants all of us to meet up sometime after you all get back, sort of like a family reunion

James: I gotta go now

**Jenn: Be safe tonight, okay?**

**James: I will**

Many Americans and Iraqis thought it would be impossible for the first Iraqi elections to take place, especially in towns such as Mosul. Some Iraqi political parties boycotted altogether. There were also terrorist groups who were kidnapping and executing political candidates compounding the election troubles. Threats of murder were made to anyone trying to vote at the polls. I think these terrorist activities and threats strengthened the resolve of Deuce Four leaders to pull off safe elections. Conducting the election successfully was important to President Bush and the leaders in Iraq, but it was the mission of Deuce Four and they don't take missions lightly.

The day after the elections I had a chance to chat with James again.

**IM- Jenn and James, February 1, 2005**

**Jenn:  Hi James - you doing okay today**

**James: Tired, but OK**

**Jenn:  I bet you've been working a lot**

**James: Yeah like from 4 am yesterday until 7am this morning**

**Jenn: Wow! seems like things went pretty well though**

**Jenn: LTC Kurilla sent a letter about some stuff that went on during the elections - good news type stuff**

James: Yeah, some places only had like 50 people vote but our site had 3000

Jenn: At least they got the opportunity to vote - you know, a lot of Americans don't vote and it's not even dangerous

James: Everyone here needs to vote

Jenn: How's your head?

James: Still hurts but that's life

Jenn: It'll take a while for you to recover

James: Yeah probably...Mail starts coming back tomorrow, now that the election is over

Jenn: Outstanding! I know it's been awhile since you got mail

Jenn: Oh, we saw your Stryker on NBC nightly news - i know it was yours because it was the day after your attack, and they said it was from that day

James: Really?

Jenn: The picture was kinda from the distance, but you could see the explosion and the Stryker jump and there was a lot of black smoke and they said the two soldiers inside were wounded, but no one was killed … it looked very scary

James: It was

Jenn: Well, i know you'll get to feeling better soon...
how's your hearing? any better?

James: No

Jenn: Well can you hear the other soldiers okay when
you are working?

James: My left ear is fine, so yes

Jenn: That's good, in the video on TV it looked like
your Stryker was going pretty slow when the bomb
went off

James: Yeah, I was going slow

Jenn: That's probably a good thing - if you'd been
going faster you might have been hurt more severely

James: Nah, I'm tough, remember?

Jenn: I know...I worry about you though...Derek
logged on yesterday and told Jon's mom that you guys
were okay, so that was nice

Jenn: But he was only on for a little bit because there
were only 2 computers available? What's going on

James: It's sucky

Jenn: Well, how is Jon?

Jenn: His mom was online looking for him earlier

James: He's fine

*conversation ended abruptly*

*During the Deuce Four deployment, there were two election issues that confronted our soldiers. The first was the United States Presidential Election of 2004, the second was Iraq's first nationwide elections on January 31, 2005.*

*Jon never got to vote. Tom and I thought he would get an absentee ballot through the Army, but it never happened.*

*Jon told us about how Deuce Four prepared for the first election in Iraq.*

**"We were actually not supposed to get involved because we didn't want the people to feel that we were in any way persuading them how to vote, making them too afraid to come out and vote, thinking they would be arrested for voting for the wrong candidate. That was their old regime. So, we were basically asked a lot of the times, to guard the areas. They could go in and vote, but we searched them before they went in and made sure they weren't going in to blow the place up. I remember the first time we were there when they were getting ready to vote. We were guarding the ballots, but we weren't allowed to pick them up and move them. They didn't want to make it seem like we were altering anything. I remember that was how one of our guys actually got injured. It was just amazing that he didn't get more injured than he was because they saw us guarding the ballots and a guy brought a bag with 3 pineapple grenades in it and pulled the pin on all 3 of them. Only 2 of the 3 blew up, but, as they hit, our guy recognized what was in it and started running away. I**

129

*remember there was an explosion and he just disappeared in the cloud. Right as the bag exploded he had jumped behind the corner of the wall and he was completely shielded. So, we were really lucky on that."*

We asked Jon what were the people like – did they seem like they wanted to vote?

*"There was some hesitation, but you could see it was really different in each neighborhood. Like old town, let's say --it was part of the old town where these buildings were just on top of each other. And, that was more of the poorer neighborhoods and they didn't really want to come out. They had a lot of fear. However, the richer neighborhoods...the places where the doctors were, or the people that owned stores, things like that, they were actually very happy to come out and vote. They had more trust. They actually thought things were going to change."*

There had been an elderly woman who came out as the first person to vote.

*"Yeah," Jon said, "we were guarding one of the places and it was weird because we had started and the polls were open for almost 2 hours, but, no one came out...no one was doing anything. And, I just remember this little old woman came out...like waddling up to us. I think they were afraid because we were standing there with guns. She didn't care. She just kind of walked in. We searched her to make sure she didn't have any bombs on her or anything like that. She went in and*

130

*voted, and I think when she walked out it kind of got everyone thinking. Well, they are not keeping us from voting, they are just trying to keep it safe. When she came out, they just started trickling in…you know one person, then a few more came down, and then finally it just got extremely crowded and when it would get too crowded we would actually break up the lines. There could be only so many people deep because we didn't want a huge group of people standing there because that just makes a huge target."*

We asked Jon if they pulled a lot of duty before the election.

*"(We monitored) a lot of the bridges. I remember one of the nights where we had spent all night, sitting on a bridge and I remember being unable to sleep the entire night. We were watching, trying to make sure no one was coming in to try to attack these buildings where the ballots were. We spent all night and of course, I was tired and cranky and just was hating life. I just remember as the sun came up there was a father. He had brought his son out and he was trying to teach him how to fly a kite and you know, his son was running and trying to get the kite up and everything and I remember that day, thinking…wow…these people are really just like us. They are just in a really crappy area. Yeah…who knows…if we had grown up in the exact same place probably we would be exactly like them."*

It makes you realize the blessing of being born in the U.S.A.

# PACKAGES

My father kept an inventory of everything he sent and numbered every package. This ritual helped keep his mind off the war. I wasn't that detailed, but I was organized. Patti and I found that assembling packages for our soldiers was very therapeutic.

Sending packages is an easy way to support the troops, but not necessarily easy to execute. Items shipped must be non-perishable and the liquids must be sealed so that they won't spill and leak during shipping. Because the climate in the combat zone can be quite different from home, you have to prepare packages with items that can withstand extreme temperature changes. And the packages may be handled quite roughly. The US Postal Services delivers all APO and FPO mail and packages to the Army mail depot. From there, the Army transports the mail to the troops in the field. This can take weeks, and packages are treated like boxes, not precious cargo. The way your packages are assembled is extremely important.

One positive side to sending packages to a soldier deployed in a combat zone is that the USPS charges the same shipping rates as if your package were being sent to an address in the United States. Of course, our boxes could get quite heavy, especially after the mess hall was bombed and we were sending a lot food to sustain our soldiers.

Non-perishable foods can be heavy, such as canned goods and cookies.

Luckily, Patti and I maintained nearly constant contact regarding not only the health and safety of our boys, but also updated each other on the packages we shipped. During the deployment the USPS introduced a flat rate priority mail box that was one charge no matter how much the box weighed. It was fantastic news! Prior to using flat rate boxes we spent hundreds of dollars on shipping packages parcel post, which can be expensive.

It really didn't matter how much we spent on packages, or how long we waited in line at the post office to ship them. To us, those packages contained love and care that we thought would lift our soldiers' spirits.

No matter what we packed in those care packages, nothing we could ship in a box would change the fact that our boys were at war. I sent my brother's favorite foods and the same brands of toiletries that he used at home. I worked hard to be creative and thoughtful. It was my hope that the care packages would make his life easier. I wanted my care packages to relieve some of his pressure.

Patti asked Jon, "How did James handle the pressure of deployment?"

Jon's answer did not shock me. It was confirmation of what I already knew. My simple, adolescent minded brother got through the war the best way he knew how. No package I could send would magically transport him home.

*Jon said, "As I remember James, he kind of joked around a lot. When he was there, at first, he was very fun to get along with pretty much the whole way there. But, as we got more an more desensitized to the explosions and the shootings and things like that, it uh, it changed him....not in the way of us...he would never do anything mean to us...but I really saw....cause I went to the phone booths and computer places with him and he completely changed the way he would talk to his sister and he would talk to other people on the phone or on the computer....and the best way I could describe it is he almost became like a spoiled brat. Um....I remember one of the times on the phone, he had gotten a package from his sister and I kind of called him on it afterwards. He was almost yelling at his sister because she sent him chips but no dip with it. And, you know, he was basically saying what kind of person sends chips and no dip, you know. You can't eat chips with no dip and things like that. It's like, Hey, you should be happy for what she gave you. And, I think it was just the pressure of being away and being on a deployment like that, and , actually being shot at. Putting yourself in a place where just overall everyone hates you there. That really changed everyone."*

That conversation sounds so callous, and it was. Callous and coarse is what James had become in order to survive. On my end of the phone I felt his emptiness...and my own because I wasn't there to help him through the toughest days of his life. James was emotionally expressing what I already knew; no care package could change where he was, what he saw, or how scared he felt. The packages I sent were my therapy. At the end of the day, I know my brother was grateful for every card, letter and care package he received.

Patti found sending packages to be therapeutic as well. As our friendship grew, we shared more with each other including the details of the packages we sent. Often we would provide each other with ideas for care packages. As we packed those boxes with care, we silently prayed that our boys would be alive to receive them. When they did, we hoped they would feel our love in the contents.

Patti asked Jon about mail call.

> *"Sometimes, I would go a couple weeks without getting anything at mail call. Some of the guys, I swear, they had a full cheer leading team, they were always getting packages, things like that. I remember James – he always had packages. It was just really the highlight of the day you know, you could slow down a bit and kind of think of the ones that you loved."*

Thanks to our IMs,Honey, and other folks in the FRG, Patti and I learned what to include in our mail, how to fill out customs slips, and how to pack our care packages. A few weeks into the deployment, our soldiers were receiving their first boxes from home.

**IM – Jenn and James, late October 2004**

135

James: Hey Jenn

Jenn: Hi you...I've been thinking about you

James: Yeah , I've been working a lot

Jenn: I hate that you have to work so much... you better get some sleep

James: Sleep what's that? A city in china?

Jenn: You're funny did you get any of my packages

James: We just got back this morning from a mission with delta and the rangers and haven't got our mail yet

Jenn: Well, maybe you'll get your second one today

James: I'm still eating the candy you sent in the first box...I've saving the rest to eat while I'm on guard tonight

Jenn: Guard duty overnight – how will you get any sleep?

James: Doesn't matter...I can't sleep here - damn terrorists...we got 2 more last night

Jenn: That's good

James: And I got to see one of the old republican guard palaces last night

Jenn: Was it really nice or what

James: Yeah it was really nice looked like someone important lived there

James: That first box you sent me had mold on it

Jenn: What kind of mold??? That's ridiculous

James: Like green mold on the outside, it was gross

Jenn: They must have let it get wet at the post office... that makes me mad

Jenn: I'll have to wrap everything in plastic...can you see my new 'worry wrinkles' on the web cam

James: Yeah, a little, ha ha... I'm fine...a lot of close calls but I'm fine

Jenn: I know...

James: I mean if you knew how close we've got a few times you would freak out

Jenn: I don't want to know...I think I know enough... there was one report on the news Sunday about some 'knock' cordons that were going on in Mosul, I don't really know what that was about, I thought it was you guys because the news said 1st brigade

James: That was us...I talked to some private security guys here at the mess hall...you wouldn't believe how well they get paid...like one guy said he paid off his house already AND they get to come home every 90 days

**Jenn: Well, that might sound great, but I don't think I want you going back to Iraq, as a soldier or a civilian**

**James: Well, I don't think I want to either, for the record**

**Jenn: I sent you a little DVD player, too – I hope you get it soon, it's wrapped in plastic and in it's box so you should get it 'mold free'**

**James: Excellent – that will be really good…hey I gotta go now…talk to you later**

---

*There really was a therapeutic nature to sending mail for the soldier's family. Mothers often talk of the "missing place" at the table at dinner time, which symbolized the gaping hole in their lives. In a way, we filled that hole with boxes. Boxes that were empty and waiting to be filled, boxes partially full, and boxes en route to the carefully scribed APO marked on the shipment. Instead of dwelling on the danger our son was in, we tried to dwell on what new, creative, "piece of home" could we send our Jon to show him our love and pride. We have always believed that if you feel out of control then do something normal. What could be more normal than preparing a box of comfort for your soldier?*

*It is curious how conversations between other soldier's family members would revolve around discussing the contents of our last care package or the one we were currently working on. Funny discussion would take place. I would say, "I sent them peanut butter," and Jenn would respond, "OH OK - I will put jelly in my next package." Or, we would realize after R&R that the smell of our soldier on the laundry brought us comfort and we let weeks pass before we could bring ourselves to wash their clothes and blankets. Then we would then sleep on a pillowcase for a week, seal it in a "Seal-a-meal" bag and send it in hopes it would give our soldier similar comfort in the familiar smell of home. We would send a little bottle of sand collected from our property hoping it would bring thoughts of the quiet serenity of our land. And at times we sent special requests like cat food, dewormer, and flea collars for the little stray cat 3rd Platoon adopted, since those items certainly would not be available on the FOB."*

*It did not matter what was sent, only that we were doing something normal, and that brought us some comfort.*

# R& R

If I had expectations for R&R, I certainly didn't expect that it would be as stressful and difficult as it was. On the contrary, I thought that the two weeks my soldier would spend at home, away from the war, would be happy and joyous. R&R for our family was nothing like that.

We had the typical R&R homecoming in the airport. I presented myself to the ticket counter and proudly accepted a security pass so that I could wait by the gate for James. As I marched through the airport, my step quickened and my heart raced. James had phoned from Atlanta, one of the U.S. entry points for soldiers returning from Iraq. At an airport bar, some businessmen had been buying soldiers drinks. James was having a good time and enjoying his first drink in a bar. He had turned 21 while in Iraq.

When I arrived at the gate, I wasn't expecting to see soldiers in the waiting area. They were with wives, girlfriends, mothers and children. They were returning to the war. My tears of joy were mirrored by tears of sadness in the eyes of those family members. I could see that in 14 short days, I too would change my hat from cheerful to somber. It was clear that the stresses of this war would not be put on hold during R&R.

I made it a point that day, as I still do now, to thank the soldiers in the waiting area for their service, to shake their hand or hug them, and to tell them that I will keep them in my prayers. All of them. Until this war is over.

Soon the plane from Atlanta landed and James disembarked with a dozen or so other soldiers from various units in Iraq, all headed to homes nearby for their R&R. There were hugs, kisses, tears, and handshakes. We whisked him away to the car; to safety and to our home.

It did not take long before I was affronted by the smell of my brother. I will never forget that smell, which could only be described as the smell of war; nauseating and depressing. Mix sweat with dirty water, diesel fuel, garbage, sulfur and charcoal and you still won't reach the magnitude of this overpowering odor. The smell was mixed with him; intertwined with his memories and experiences. I washed those fatigues 4 times, and I still could not eliminate it completely. Some things just cannot be washed away.

We stopped on the way home at a cafeteria-style restaurant that my brother just loves. He was still in his smelly fatigues, but we didn't care. It was one of the best meals any of us have ever had. James loaded up on mashed potatoes, roast beef, ice cream, pop…all sorts of food. Lots of folks eating lunch in the restaurant smiled at us and a few came over to thank James for his service. It was the happiest time of those two weeks, and of that whole year.

141

While home, James spent much of his time online chatting with his brother soldiers back in Mosul. This was very surprising. I expected him to disconnect from the war during his time home, but he did the opposite. I could tell that he was worried about his friends, and that staying connected to them via the internet was his way of making sure they would still be around when he returned to Mosul.

R&R was stressful for me, too.

Before my brother came home for his two week 'vacation', he started chatting with me about his faith, our church, and the possibility of counseling. James expressed interest in talking to our pastor about the war and his experiences. Obviously, he was reaching out for help. I phoned our pastor and told him about James' request. I expected the pastor to embrace our request with passion. This was not the case. Our pastor told me that he would be uncomfortable counseling James about the war. I remember him actually saying, "I've just never been good at counseling." Unbelievable. Our pastor suggested that I phone the regional church office to see if they had someone qualified to counsel James. I never did. I was so put off by the pastor's inadequate response that I became bitter toward him, our church, and to some degree, even my faith. Looking back, I wish I had pursued James' request for counseling more vigorously.

My son's grade school class had been writing to James and his fellow soldiers during the deployment, so during R&R

142

my brother visited the class. I accompanied him that day to serve as moral support and to help guide him through the many questions we were sure the children would ask.

While on one of his many patrols, James 'visited' the border of Iraq and Syria. He never told me if his platoon actually crossed the border into Syria, but he did bring home some Syrian money. The bills were interesting and certainly unique. We made copies of the Syrian bills and some worthless Iraqi money and handed them out to the children. The class made a banner for James, too. It was red, white, and blue and hung on the door to the classroom.

When we arrived, the teacher introduced James and the children clapped for him. It was bittersweet. Seeing the children admiring a soldier and celebrating their patriotism was wonderful, but it occurred to me that these children could not remember a time when our nation was not at war.

James prepared a small speech about Deuce Four and the work they were doing in Iraq, such as helping train the Iraqi Army and Police Force and providing security for the streets so that the people could travel to work and school safely. After he spoke, the teacher asked the children if anyone had questions. Many little hands flung into the air. Is it hot there? What do Iraqi people eat? Have you ever seen a scorpion? These were some of the questions.

143

Then, an innocent child asked the inevitable question. Have you killed anyone? I knew before we even set foot in the school that this question would be asked so I prepared my brother.

"What do you think you should say if one of the children asks you about killing?" I questioned my brother in the car on the way to the school.

"I dunno. What do you think I should say?" he replied.

I did not think it was appropriate for him to tell children about killing, even though the circumstances were those of war. I carefully constructed an answer that would be truthful but not graphic.

"If you are asked about killing, simply say that war is tough and sometimes people die. Children do not need gory details, so keep your answer short and move on."

That is exactly how James answered the question. He stared straight at me as he delivered the line we practiced in the car. I smiled slightly to reassure him until the next child asked a question and we moved on. Soon the visit ended and the class gathered around their soldier pen pal and we snapped a photo. Looking back, I think it was wrong to take James to the school. While he handled himself well, and the children were thrilled to meet one of the soldiers they had been writing, James was too raw from battle. It did not occur to me that he had seen small children that same age killed in front of him, victims of

144

war. If I had it to do all over again, that visit to the school would not have taken place.

I knew that James was home safe, but I could not help but dread his return to Iraq and fear for his safety when he was away from home. One night, James stayed away from home all night partying. When he returned the next day he was severely hung over; so impaired in fact that he did not move from bed the whole day. I took him water, aspirin and sports drinks hoping to bring him around. When he did emerge from his stupor, I noticed scratches on his face and arms. I asked him about this and his reply was that he had fallen down. While that was possible, it was not likely. In my mind, I imagined that he had been in a fight, perhaps targeted at a bar in our liberal college town because he was a combat soldier. I did not press him for details; he probably did not even remember. I will never know what happened that night. What I did know was that my brother was not the same as before he left for Iraq.

We had hoped to visit Ft. Knox while James was home on R&R so he could see a hearing specialist, maybe get a hearing aid. I secretly wanted the Army to examine him and determine that having a deaf driver in combat was a really bad idea and then forbid him from returning to Iraq, but I guess being able to hear wasn't that big of a deal to the Army. I asked our family physician about examining him, but in the short two weeks that James was home there wasn't enough time for appointments and testing. James didn't even seem very interested in fixing his hearing trouble, so we let it go.

145

The day we returned my brother to the airport for the end of R&R I did not cry. I could not cry. It was harder for me than anything had ever been in my life. I knew exactly where he was going and what the future might hold for us: that we might not have a future together. As the rest of my family made small talk during the hour-long drive to the airport, I mostly stared out the window. I bit my tongue, I pinched my arms; I did anything I could to keep my mind sharp and my tears at bay.

I did not walk my brother to the gate. I gave him a quick hug, told him I loved him and to be safe, and then nearly sprinted to the car. I wanted it to be as easy as possible for him to leave.

---

*R&R was promised to all the US soldiers sent to IRAQ with long deployments. Of course, the Army cannot just shut down for vacation when in a war zone, so the timing of R&R for each individual soldier was not fixed and was subject to the usual whimsical changes of Army life.*

*The thought of R&R for our soldiers is sort of a cross between Christmas coming, a Las Vegas vacation, and a spiritual pilgrimage to the "promised land". No real life experience would stand a chance against those high expectations built up over months of dreaming.*

*The families at home tend to have their own blown out of proportion dreams of their dear sweet soldier returning to the bosom of the family for two wonderful weeks of relaxation. Likewise, the family expectations are unrealistic.*

*All R&R experiences are different, but none of them are pure sweetness and light. This is the time that we have to face the fact that our soldiers have been changed and will never be the way they were again. As I look over the photos of Jon's R&R I am reminded that the mouth smiled but the eyes told the truth. Grey circles of weariness, no sparkle of hope, only dullness from having seen way too much misery, unjustness, and death at such a young age.*

*Originally, Jon thought he would be getting R&R in March or April. But of course, this was the original planning, before such things as injuries, babies being born to soldiers at war, unplanned family emergencies, and the strain on Pilots and Airplanes caused by Hurricane Katrina could be factored into the equation.*

*This felt like whimsical changes to the families who would try to arrange vacation at work, make travel arrangements for far away family members who wanted to see our soldier - only to have the date change again and again at the last minute. We were fortunate that Jon's R&R came after those of others in our circle of Army friends and family, so that by the time May 2005 finally rolled around and became the timing for Jon's R&R we had a "Wait 'til you see the whites of his eyes" approach to our celebration planning.*

*And, by this time, Ashley and Jon had become an "item", talking often online.*

147

*IM - Patti and Jon, Spring 2005*

*Jon:    Ashley has been chatting with me a lot. It is nice talking to her.*

*Patti: Well, she says she enjoys talking with you. Of course, I told her you were a GREAT guy.*

*Jon:    Good! I still have her fooled!*

*We knew if we were to see much of Jon during R&R that Ashley would have to be part of the planning. Tom and I have always had a practical approach to our son's behaviors and we knew Parents would play a POOR second choice to a 23 year-old healthy male that had been starved of female attention for more than six months. In addition, we had become close online friends with Ashley and we also really wanted to get to know her better. Ashley was invited to come to our home for the entire two weeks that Jon would be here and celebrate with us his return home.*

*To add to our challenges, Tom, Jon's dad and my husband, contracted pneumonia just before Jon returned home on R&R and had been weak, tired, and uncomfortable. Our planning and arrangements had to be done working around the complication of his illness.*

*Ashley arrived at Tucson International Airport the day before Jon was due to arrive. Now mind you, we really did not have an exact time to work with. Jon thought he would be leaving at a certain time, but there is a bit of a blackout period as our soldiers go from their regular quarters to a staging area, then they are sent to Kuwait, and finally they are flown to a European refueling spot. SO the time of arrival is an estimate until they finally land in their first US location and the actual domestic flight they will be on becomes known.*

*We sort of knew Jon was on his way from IMs from other soldiers like Derek (who was still waiting for his R&R) and James (who had just returned from his R&R). What they knew was that Jon had gone to the initial staging area and James estimated timing for us based upon his journey.*

*We could guesstimate better when Jon called from Ireland. This was a surprise because James had gone through Germany, but, for some reason Jon's plane stopped in Ireland for refueling. We learned later that there was a fairly lengthy layover in Ireland, many of our soldiers were putting large amounts of alcohol into their unprepared bodies that had been without alcohol for many, many months. Without the aid of wheel chairs pushed by slightly less inebriated buddies, some would not have made it back to their plane!*

*Tom, Chris, our youngest, and I met Ashley at the airport. She was so pretty and sweet, our small fears of complications melted away instantly. She was just as wonderful in person as she had been by phone and IM. We knew she would make Jon's R&R as enjoyable as it was possible to be.*

*The next day, Jon was arriving, Ashley, Tommy, Jeremy, a childhood friend, Bibiana, a neighbor girl and I went to the airport. Tom was so weak from his illness, he could not go. We put a yellow ribbon bow on the front of the car, and each of us put a yellow ribbon on some part of our body. Ashley and Bibiana had their's tied as a bow on their necks. Tommy refused any spot except his wrist. We parked the car and went inside as far as we were allowed to enter to meet Jon in the terminal.*

*As Jon walked down the hallway leading to where we were, we all started waving and shouting. Bystanders were smiling and moving out of the way to give us room. It was heartwarming how supportive Americans, who just happened to share the same space at the same time, were of us and our soldier. It was a cheerful and memorable homecoming.*

*Shortly after the initial excitement ebbed, we noticed a strange smell. Jon told us that this is just the way everything smells in Iraq. Some sort of mix between sewage and cabbage cooking. As soon as we got home, and Tom and Jon greeted each other, Jon stripped of his BDUs and gave me all his clothes. We washed them and washed them - five times to get the smell to a tolerable level. Fortunately, I had been warned by Jenn, who had already experienced this so it was no big shock and we just took care of the problem.*

*Jon had brought gifts for each of us. He had a specially made hat for his dad and marble goblets for me. He was so proud to have been able to bring gifts home for us, and we were enormously proud of our son and brother. The stories he told us were fascinating but shocking. He was transformed into a survivor with a strong theme of "it's them or me, and it is NOT going to be me that gets shot". He had little to say that was positive of Iraq, and nothing positive to say about the Army and the war experience. He was bone tired, discouraged, and would have seized on any opportunity not to go back, but there were none.*

*The next two weeks zoomed by. I had to work most of the time, but Ashley and Tom kept Jon happily occupied. They did a nice mix of just relaxing and sightseeing so Ashley could learn a little about our desert in southern Arizona. Tom and I took them to Nogales, Mexico one day for sightseeing and they were so comfortable and happy together. We did have one big party for family and friends, but looking back on it I think it made Jon uncomfortable and perhaps in hindsight I would not do that again. We all pretty successfully ignored the nagging realization that the days were passing fast and it would soon be time for Jon to return to HELL. That is what our soldiers called the war zone to which they were assigned.*

*The morning he had to return I was scheduled to work. I could have taken the day off but I knew I could not be the supportive, brave, tear-free mom I should be if I went to the airport. So I said goodbye in the driveway, as Tom, Ashley, and Tommy boarded the Suburban and took him to the airport. I still tear up thinking of it. He was GONE again. To fight a war he did not believe in. Would he return? There was no way to know.*

# WHERE IS JON?

I know of soldiers' families who go months without hearing from their loved one stationed in Iraq. Unless you have contact with an FRG, the only way you can get information about the war is from CNN or online news reports.

This type of disconnection happened to a friend of mine during her husband's second deployment. After coming home five months in for his R&R, he seemed distant and cold. After the soldier returned to duty, his wife and parents didn't hear from him for over seven months. One day, he showed up in his fatigues, driving a rental car, with no explanation and no apologies. It seemed the only way he could get through his deployment was to completely withdraw.

There was a time during the deployment that Jon disconnected from his family. Fortunately, the disconnect didn't last long. During that time I did my best to ask my brother about Jon and to relay messages from Jon's folks back to him through James.

When Jon's communication block ended, I received a short, but happy email from my dear friend.

*Jenn - Just a quick message...we IM'd with Jon today. Thank you for your help in getting James to push him back online. Happy day! TTYL – Patti*

*During R&R we spent every moment we could with our son,
wanting to be there to comfort and support. After two weeks of
being able to know he was safely sleeping in our home, the shock
and worry of having him far away, with no way of knowing
when or IF we would talk to him again was depressing. But
there was no time for us to wallow in depression; it soon became
clear Jon needed us to pull him out of HIS depression.*

*Imagine returning to HELL after two weeks of relative paradise,
with four to five months of war duty ahead of you.
Understandably, several weeks went by with no contact.
Fortunately, we had the IM contact list with several of Jon's war
buddies.....so when we would see them online, we would ask
how he was doing. Mostly they said he was OK, but in his
"hooch" playing XBOX. At least we knew he was OK. After a
few weeks of worry, I mentioned what I guessed was Jon's
depression to Jenn. Jenn asked her brother James to get Jon to
come to the Computer center to IM with us. Finally after
several days of coaxing, one night there he was. What a relief we
felt to have our communication link reconnected.*

*I cannot fully explain how critical our networking with Jenn,
James, Derek and our entire Army family had become. Without
them, we could have suffered silence and separation for months,
just as the family Jenn described earlier did during the
separation from their soldier. We were, and are, so grateful for
Jon's return to us.*

*Why were we so afraid and troubled over Jon's depression and lack of communication?*

*We were very aware that the suicide rate in Iraq was growing – not from public reports, but from the words and feelings we received through contact with our son and his battle buddies. At that time, in 2005, not a lot was being said publicly.....but we sensed the rise in danger studied in 2007 and reported in 2008. In an article dated Feb 3, 2008, titled "Concern mounts over rising troop suicides." The article was startling.*

> *In 2007, five soldiers per day attempted suicide*

> *Legislation has been introduced by Senator Jim Webb of Virginia to improve soldier care*

> *Soldiers must overcome stigma of treatment, said an Army psychiatrist. "We know that soldiers don't want to seek care"*

> *Suicide attempts are rising and have risen over the last five years." -Col. Elspeth Cameron-Ritchie, Army psychiatrist*

*Concern over the rate of suicide attempts prompted Sen. Jim Webb, D-Virginia, to introduce legislation to improve the military suicide-prevention programs.*

*"Our troops and their families are under unprecedented levels of stress due to the pace and frequency of more than five years of deployments," Webb said in a written statement.*

*We resumed chatting online with Jon every week to 10 days. Little by little, he seemed to show signs of pulling out of his* depression, but he was never happy. He just forced himself to keep on going with the goal of returning to the "world" as his motivation. Our contact was not frequent. We learned early on that it was best to start our communication with greetings of LOVE and pride in Jon's service to us and to his country. You never knew when the communication would break. Sometimes it was a sudden attack that pulled the soldiers away. Sometimes it was a comrade who had been killed and communication was instantly cut. Various unplanned and frustrating things could cause the instant messaging to be cut off in mid-sentence.

By this time, we had also learned that the easiest way to keep all our interested friends and family up on what was going on with Jon in Iraq was to forward them a copy of our instant messages. They loved being able to "eavesdrop" on our conversations and got a new appreciation of what it really means to have a loved one involved in a war. In modern war, technology has pulled the soldiers' families into the midst of the pain, suffering, and lunacy of war. One would think it would teach all of us to avoid deadly conflict and seek methods of diplomacy to solve differences. How strange that those who make the decision to sacrifice our sons, have little to no direct connection to the suffering, pain and lifelong loss that it causes.

From R&R forward, each day was another day marked off the calendar until the time Deuce Four would come home. That too was an estimate that changed with the times and needs of the all – consuming war. We tried to ignore this, pick a "reasonable" date and do our countdown as if it were real.

*Our routines helped us to stay sane. Every trip to the store included a search for something new that our third Platoon "sons" would like. Planning for the next package, thinking up something creative, preparing the box, and delivering it to the post office every Saturday before noon when it closed, was the mind-saving ritual for me and my other Army family support system members, such as Jenn, Ashley, Lisa (Derek's step mom), Jessy (Derek's fiancée) and so on. It was quite simply, the ONLY thing we could do to help.*

*During this stage of deployment, time passed slowly, worry was high, and we prayed incessantly. Normal Life was on HOLD. We forgot to see the doctor, postponed and never reset dental appointments, avoided any activity that would remove us from "mission control center"-- our computers and telephones. To miss a call or to realize that our soldier had been online and we didn't see them was heartbreaking. Up to this point of my life, I had no real knowledge of the strength that career military spouses have. I now know that the good ones are like the Rock of Gibraltar and ~~have~~ they have my undying respect.*

*One such pillar of strength was Honey Bartel, our FRG Family Resource Guide.*

# HONEY

Honey is God's nectar and has been a necessary and important part of life for thousands of years. The human form of Honey, as in Honey Bartel, was without a doubt the "medicine" that I needed to get me through some tough times during deployment.

Honey contacted me just days into the deployment. Her husband Matt was the sergeant in charge of the A-Company, 3$^{rd}$ Platoon. Prior to deployment, Honey and Matt asked the single soldiers for contact information if they wanted their loved ones to receive updates as regularly as the wives of married soldiers staying on base at Ft. Lewis. Every unmarried soldier gave Honey the name and contact information for someone they loved, be it a mother, sister, aunt, or girlfriend.

Wives staying on base during the deployment were able to attend FRG meetings, and had more opportunities for involvement and information. For families of soldiers living away from the base, in my case 2,300 miles away from Ft. Lewis, there was no way to be in touch with other Deuce Four family members unless you were added to the FRG email list. What Honey did for me and Patti by adding us to the FRG email list was nothing short of angelic. To be included in the Deuce Four electronic dispatches sent from FOB Marez was so vital to our well-being.

157

Thanks to Honey, even when our soldiers withdrew and we could not email or instant message, we still received communication from the FRG and Deuce Four officers. We knew what was going on with the battalion. At times, this information was the only thing that could suppress our anxiety and easy the tension we felt at home.

It seemed that Honey was holding it together for all of us. Years after the Deuce Four deployment to Mosul ended I told Honey how I saw her as a really strong woman. She said to me, "I never would have guessed that I had it in me." That is how we all felt, really. Our soldiers never realized how much stress, death and destruction they could handle. At the same time, the families back home never realized how much agony, sorrow and fear they could manage.

Honey knew she was in a position to make a difference during the deployment as the wife of a platoon sergeant. Many of the girlfriends and family members had already met Honey while visiting the soldiers at Ft. Lewis, and the men in the platoon trusted her just as they did their sergeant. Even though Honey never met us, she gave us her all.

*As with every deployment, a group of soldiers from Deuce Four known as the rear detachment or Rear D, stayed at Ft. Lewis to keep operations running and to maintain connections with the soldiers' families through what is known as a Family Readiness Group, or FRG. When important information about Deuce Four needed to be relayed to the families, an officer from Rear D would contact the leaders of the FRG who would in turn email and phone family members both at Ft. Lewis and across the country. This source of information was priceless to us during the deployment. Honey Bartel served as our FRG.*

*Honey was married to 3ʳᵈ Platoon Sergeant Bartel. She was assigned to the single men of Deuce Four, A-Company. Jon had never given our contact information to the Army before he deployed, but fortunately, James had done so. Since James was also single, this meant Jenn was aware of the FRG and she gave me Honey's contact information. I contacted Honey and Tom and I were added to the email contact list. This was helpful because Honey would send out the official notices to us. Often we would receive a memo from the captain who would speak to the overall status of the group or advise of the loss of soldiers and the circumstance of their brave deaths. She was also part of the planning for the welcoming of Deuce Four when they returned. The wives and girlfriends of the soldiers who were in the Ft. Lewis, Washington area did an outstanding job of helping to make the barracks clean, decorated and welcoming for the returning single soldiers.*

*Honey offered to let us send new sheets, and a pillow for Jon's bunk in the barracks to her home. Ashley made up Jon's bed and decorated his room. She gave Jon a comforter to match the sheets and pillow we had sent. A goodie bag of cookies and personal items were put on the bed, and a huge banner from our church members with everyone's signature and greeting was hung on the wall of his room by Ashley.*

*Knowing Ashley and Jenn would be there to welcome our guys home was a huge comfort for us since we could not be at the homecoming. Later, Tom and I returned the favor, when we attended the Redeployment Ceremony and Jenn could not attend.*

# HOLDING OUR BREATH

There was a lot more going on with Deuce Four than anything published in the headlines. It is difficult to communicate with well meaning friends, family and even strangers who just do not understand how difficult war deployments are on families back home. Standing in line one day at the post office, a woman asked me where I was sending my stack of packages. I replied that they were intended for James and other soldiers in Mosul, Iraq.

"Oh dear," she replied, "I know just what you are going through. My niece is stationed in Kuwait and it's just hell worrying about her every day." What! You've GOT to be kidding me, I thought to myself. This woman's niece would be in more danger at the local mall than in Kuwait. Why don't you think about what life would be like if your niece were worried every second of every day that she would be hit by a mortar or drive over an IED or be gunned down in the street? I just looked at her, said nothing, turned back around in line and waited for the next postal teller so that I could get the hell out of there.

Strangers weren't the only ones to make seemingly callous remarks. Members of my church at the time would often say to me, "I don't know how you keep it together so well." You know what, neither did I. What I am going to do, get into bed for the next year and let the rest of my life go to hell? I keep it together because my soldier is keeping it together every day while being targeted by terrorists with suicide missions. My life is a cake walk and so is yours.

The hardest question to confront was always the one about killing. "Has James had to kill anyone?" Hum, let's see, he served in over 500 combat missions in less than a year in one of the most dangerous cities in the world. WHAT THE HELL DO YOU THINK?!

As we dealt with the worry and anxiety, the deployment began to near the finish line. Our boys were anxious to come home, but also had to deal with the task of training their replacements. We asked Jon about what it was like when the other battalion arrived and prepared to take over operations.

> *"There was a difference between what we did and what Alaska did when they took over. One of the first problems was that they brought their own vehicles so you could tell a big difference between us and them. They also switched to a different uniform, and they didn't want to search as many vehicles or kick in as many doors as us. They really wanted to pull guard around the FOB and you know, not really roll out and do anything. They wanted the ING to start doing that work. Of course, if you rely on anyone else to get something done, it's not going to get done correctly."*

Even though Deuce Four had fought hard, they would leave with much left to be done.

# REDEPLOYMENT

Deuce Four was originally a unit of one of the first Buffalo Soldier regiments in the United States Army along with the 9th and 10th Cavalries. They were involved in the Spanish-American War and were with Teddy Roosevelt's Rough Riders' famous charge up San Juan Hill.

They were assigned to the 1st Brigade, 25th Infantry Division 'Lightning' (a Stryker brigade), and served in Iraq from October 2004 to September 2005. Along with many other medals, the Battalion came home with 181 Purple Hearts and played a crucial role in the Battle of Mosul. During that battle, the Battalion saw some of the heaviest, sustained fighting of the insurgency to date. The unit was also awarded with the Valorous Unit.

The unit was re-flagged as the 3rd Squadron, 2nd Stryker Cavalry Regiment and moved to Vilseck, Germany after returning from Iraq in 2005. Deuce Four is now decommissioned. Stryker Brigade Combat Teams remain in Ft. Wainwright, Alaska and Schofield Barracks, Hawaii.

I could not attend the redeployment ceremony, which was held in October when all members of Deuce Four had returned to Ft. Lewis from Iraq. Patti was not able to attend the actual Homecoming Ceremony for our boys, which was held the day their company returned. So we took turns representing the Smith/Donahue family.

163

The hardest part about homecoming is ironically the same as the hardest part of the deployment itself – waiting. For months, the dates of the actual homecoming from Iraq had shifted and rescheduled. The travel itself was difficult because coordinating enough planes for the men and their equipment proved to be challenging for even the most seasoned Army officers. There's also the matter of security to consider, as terrorists would love nothing more than to take down a plane of battle weary soldiers leaving the front.

I booked airfare and hotel accommodations on a prayer that the soldiers would return while I was at Ft. Lewis. Four days after my arrival it looked as if I might have to extend my stay because the homecoming was delayed even more. We were given a website address to check every few hours. It would list the platoons that would be arriving on the next flight in. I checked, checked, and rechecked, with no sign of our soldiers. It was maddening. I found myself jealous of the families with soldiers already on flights home. How ridiculous to feel that way. I knew my soldier was out of harms way, safely awaiting a flight in Kuwait. Nevertheless, I found the endless hours of waiting nearly unbearable.

On Friday September 23rd, we emailed James from our hotel room near Ft. Lewis.

**Hello James,**

**Dad and I arrived safely today around Noon. We picked up our rental car and checked into the hotel, which is just down from the main gate at Ft. Lewis. Dad and I have been sightseeing and anxiously await your return. We are so relieved that you are safe in Kuwait and will be home soon.**

**Although we can't wait to see you, we know it may be a few days. That's okay. We just want you to know how much we love you and how proud of you we are. Take care and we'll see you very soon!**

**Love and big hugs,**

**Jenn**

Finally, on Monday September 26<sup>th</sup>, my brother's platoon was listed on the manifest; our boys would be safely in the U.S. in just hours.

I traveled through the Ft. Lewis gate, proudly displaying the family homecoming pass in my rental car window. The homecoming ceremony was held in what can best be described as an old school gymnasium, lined with bleachers on one end, a large garage door on the other end, and an empty, glossy hardwood floor in between . Soon, our boys would be marched in and presented to us in nothing less than grand fashion.

A large screen was set up across from the bleachers with photos of Deuce Four soldiers during their deployment, and memorials to those who had fallen. As the photos began to display, I noticed a nice couple sitting next me

165

began to become very upset. It was an emotional experience and there were certainly no dry eyes in the place. I leaned over, smiled, and asked, "Are you waiting for your son?"

"No," they replied.

Then, my eye caught a glimpse of dog tags clenched tightly in the woman's hand.

"Our soldier won't be coming home."

Suddenly my heart stopped and then ached with such pain that I could barely utter, "I'm sorry." I felt so selfish and shallow. Why was I bothered so much by waiting a few extra days for the homecoming when so many families would always be waiting for a homecoming that will never come?

The bleachers hummed with excitement as we waited, and waited, and waited. It seemed like our soldiers would never arrive. Children were running all over the gymnasium, newborn babies wailed as they waited to meet their daddies...some for the very first time. All sorts of balloons and homemade signs covered the gym, and some families wore matching shirts all in one color so that their soldier could easily find them in the crowd.

An announcer came over the loud speaker and the crowd immediately hushed. They had arrived, were in formation just outside the gymnasium, and in a moment the door would be lifted. Our boys would march into the gym, and

166

after a short ceremony they would be released to their families.

After they marched in, and were released, there was a mad rush to the floor. More hugging and kissing than I had ever seen. The worst part for us, was that my father and I are both so short we couldn't see through the sea of people to find our soldier. After looking for several minutes, we decided to return to the bleachers and wait for him to find us. Which he did, and it was wonderful. We went to dinner with James, Jon, Ashley and other friends. There were lots of smiles. When we returned to the hotel from dinner, I sent an email with the homecoming news.

**Dear friends and family,**

**This is my official email...James has returned from Iraq! Thank you everyone for your prayers, emails, phone calls, and support during the past year (actually, 341 days – and yes, we were counting). Words cannot express how grateful I am for the support so many of you have provided. Many times during the past year you have given me a soft place to land, to complain or cry, to gripe and moan, and for that I am truly grateful. James wants me to let you know how much he appreciates the many cards, letters and packages that were sent to him in Iraq. Finally, our family asks that you continue to pray for our soldiers abroad and for our nation. While James' homecoming was wonderful, the bittersweet reality is that not everyone came home, and there were parents**

at the ceremony who went home today with only dog tags. I thank God for bringing home James, and I thank each of you for your prayers and support.

God Bless You,

Jennifer MackInday

---

*We asked Jon about to tell us about the debriefing that is given to redeployed soldiers.*

"Really, there is some, but it's as you are coming back through, you are waiting in line, and you are stuck trying to get all your shots, everything done at once. And it's an entire day event of waiting in this line, and this line, and making sure you had health insurance, you didn't want to increase this. It really gives you a headache. It's not an individual thing. It's all just mass slamming you through this. Then they basically tell you at the end of the day you are free for the rest of the day to do anything, so, your incentive is to go through real quick and say, hey there is nothing really wrong with me, just so you can get it signed off and stamped off real quick so you can get out of there and go party and do whatever you want like be with your loved ones. So I really don't think that they sit down with a lot of the soldiers that are redeploying and really talk to them to see if they have troubles, and it is very hard for them to do that. I had to talk to a lot of guys that were coming back and had problems and you know, *just being their medic. We built a trust since while we were there, that they could show or tell me anything."*

Jenn graciously shared with us by phone and email describing the events of the Homecoming for Deuce Four. At the time, I was working, it was late in the year, and I was not able to get vacation days without at least a month's notice. The uncertainty of the arrival date made it impossible for us to be there for their return day. We were so relieved, as Jenn described each event that unfolded over the several days she and her father waited for our soldier's return to U.S. soil.

It was comforting to know that our soldiers had volunteer greeters at the first airport they reached in the U.S.A. There are greeters in Bangor, Maine and Dallas, Texas, who have made sure NOT ONE landing plane of troops from Iraq have been left unattended. They are dedicated Patriots to whom I will always be grateful. Perhaps you have heard about these wonderful volunteers and thought that is nice. When you are the parent of a soldier returning from a year-long deployment it is MUCH more than nice. It is one of the soothing thoughts that comforted us and keep us sane. To realize that other Americans, perhaps a Vietnam Vet, or another mother in a different state, will be cheering your son, shaking his hand, giving him the hug you so desperately want to deliver or handing him a cell phone to call you.....it's a huge kindness.

Thanks to Ashley, who had made sure Jon had a cell phone in his room ready for the moment he was allowed to call us, we heard from him soon after he landed. During the first few weeks of Jon's return, we talked every day. Often only for a few minutes, *just to hear his voice was a wonderful blessing. The small things we usually take for granted, like being free to call our son, were exciting and new, those first few days.*

*Soon, the timing for the Redeployment Ceremony was known. It would be held October 27, 2005, at Ft. Lewis. Quickly we determined that Tom, Tommy, Jon's older brother, and I would be going. At that time, I was active in a support group called Proud Army Moms or PAM. I posted to the support group that we would be going and asked if any other mothers would be there.*

*Peggy Alexander, the Mother of Christian Alexander, a Lieutenant in the 73rd Engineering Group attached to the Stryker Brigade, responded. Peggy and I didn't know each other well...we had just seen each others names in the PAM Message posting, but she called me. At first Peggy said that she would like to go but probably wouldn't, but after a few phone calls, she began to change her mind. In the end, Peggy did attend, and we were able to spend a very nice day together at Ft. Lewis.*

*I was so proud of Jon, and so happy to be able to share this emotional time with my husband Tom and son Tommy. I describe the Redeployment events but I fear I will not be able to adequately describe the level of emotion and inspiration that we felt as they unfolded.*

*We arrived the evening before the ceremony was scheduled. Tom and I had rented a car, but Jon and Ashley drove up to the airport anyway to meet us and to transport us and our luggage to the off-site rental car agency that we had selected. Now this was a comical site. None of us in the Donahue clan are exactly small. Jon is 6 ft 5 in, Tom is 6 ft 2 in, Tommy is 6 ft, and both Ashley and I are 5 ft 8 in. Jon's car was a two-door Honda Civic. Five large people, with luggage for three, made for a "Keystone Cop" type loading process. Fortunately, the rental agency was not very far away and we did make it just fine...laughing all the way. It was a happy way to begin our adventure.*

*Once we completed the rental car paperwork and loaded up we were on our way South from Seattle Tacoma Airport to the Ft. Lewis area.*

*Thanks to Jenn, we found a great hotel that was very near Ft. Lewis, reasonably priced, and very convenient. There were many families in the hotel, for the Redeployment Ceremony and other activities taking place at Ft. Lewis. Our hotel had a Jacuzzi and all of us enjoyed relaxing soaks several times.*

*We knew that Jon and Ashley had been becoming closer and closer friends over the last month, but we soon learned they were in love. It seemed Jon was spending almost all his free time at Ashley's parents' house. Of course, we were delighted.*

*The following day, Ashley joined us at the hotel. Jon was required to be on the post for early formation and ceremony preparations. The four of us had breakfast at the hotel, and then we went to the parade grounds. It was a lovely day, just a bit windy, but sunny and pleasant. QUITE a blessing in the state of Washington, where rain is so plentiful.*

*We found our way to the bleachers. I was scanning the crowd looking for Peggy, but never did find her there. Soon, the*

171

*various Companies that made up the 1ˢᵗ Brigade, 25ᵗʰ JD,*
*assembled on the huge, grassy field.*

*If you have never witnessed 5,000 troops assembled on one large*
*parade ground, it is an AWESOME sight. Picking out your son,*
*even a tall one like ours, is impossible. The ceremony lasted*
*about an hour. The bleachers were filled with people of all ages*
*and descriptions. The excitement of the crowd was palpable.*

## AGENDA
**Invocation by Chaplain**
**Formation of Troops**
**Honors**
**Inspection of Troops**
**National Anthem**
**Un-casing of the colors**
**Remembrance of Fallen Comrades**
**Salute to the Wounded**
**Various Remarks by dignitaries**
**Retiring of the Colors**
**First Corps & Army Song**

*As you would imagine, the Remembrance of Fallen Comrades*
*was memorable and very sad. To my surprise, my heart felt even*
*heavier when the Salute to the Wounded began. There, before our*
*eyes, were many, many young wounded soldiers. Some in*
*wheelchairs being pushed by limping comrades, blind soldiers*
*being led by others, amputees on crutches proudly assembling*
*before us, and all bearing terrible burdens for the remainder of*
*their lives. We owe these soldiers, and all the wounded heroes*
*they represent, SO MUCH, and our country gives them SO*
*LITTLE. We pray this will change. It MUST.*

172

*After the ceremony, we drove to Hangar 3025 where the Lancer Brigade Soldier & Family Redeployment Bash was being held. As we made our way there, I was able to reach Peggy on the cell phone. We agreed on a meeting spot, and soon we were together.*

*Jon stayed with us the entire time. Patiently showing us the Strykers on display, helping his mom and Peggy into the driver's hatch, and in general being a great host for all of us. Periodically, we would call Jenn and try to keep her posted on the events going. We invited James to join us there, and for several other events, but he preferred his own activities.*

*Somewhat to our surprise, it was much the same for Peggy. Her Christian told her he had to work. Jon sort of "raised his eyebrows" but said nothing. Years later, Jon confided in me that NO ONE in Lancer Brigade had to work that day.*

*It is important to realize that each soldier heals his hidden wounds in his own way and on his own time schedule. Their loved ones must understand and avoid taking their need for quiet time or peace alone as a slight, but rather as a necessary medicine. Peggy wisely understood, spent the day with us, and allowed her son the space he needed. I learned a lot from Peggy that day and have tried to apply that patience and understanding to other occasions.*

*The commanders of Deuce Four put on a great party. There were static displays of Stryker vehicles that we were allowed to crawl over and sit in with our soldiers, who proudly described their features. There were MOUNTAINS of food, hamburgers, hot*

173

*dogs, chips, drinks, live bands, clowns, face painters, and several football and basketball events.*

*We stayed long enough to eat, learn about the Stryker vehicles, and to meet LTC Erik Kurilla. What a treat that was. He was still using crutches, healing from his multiple gun shot injuries, and we know he was in pain, but he did not let on a hint of that. He shook our hands, told us proudly of our son's bravery, and clearly demonstrated the leader that he is. LTC Kurilla was the last soldier wounded from the Stryker Brigade prior to the end of their deployment.*

*Over the next couple of days, we relaxed with Jon and Ashley. One evening we had dinner with Ashley's family. Another evening we enjoyed dinner at their home. We went to Fisherman's Warf and the Space Needle. Dan Stahle, another of Jon's platoon-mates joined us. Near the end of our stay we attended a party held for 3$^{rd}$ platoon at Matt and Honey Bartel's home. It was such a wonderful day. We got to meet the young men we had come to love as adopted sons over the last year. We enjoyed a barbecue and some fabulous dishes prepared by Honey's mom. Meeting Honey, SFC Bartel, and their beautiful daughter Olivia, was a privilege.*

*Jenn's brother James did attend that party. We were glad we finally did get to spend a little time with him. Also there was Derek Young and his new bride Jessy. They were vibrant in their newlywed happiness. It was a perfect ending to our short visit. I highly recommend attending a Redeployment Ceremony. It is very inspiring.*

*On December 16, 2004, Jon and Ashley wed. We were unable to be there for their wedding in person, but we did attend via the cell phone in Jon's jacket pocket. Jon called us just before the ceremony began. We had hoped to be able to set up web cams for watching, but it just was not possible. At the last second my husband Tom said to Jon, "Just put your phone in your pocket, we will go on MUTE and listen in." It was wonderful for Tom and me, lying in bed , our heads pressed close together, listening to our son's wedding vows. Ashley did not even realize we were listening in until after the ceremony when Jon removed the phone from his jacket and said it was time to say hello to her new mom and dad.*

*Since then, Jon and Ashley have presented us with the two most beautiful babies in the world, Grace and Reagan. They are one year apart, full of life and energy, and Tom and I are completely in love with them.*

# PTSD

I find my path crossing those of young war veterans quite often. It is strange really, but I suppose these encounters are meant to be part of my healing. In 2008, I met a young man, around age 25, who served in Iraq escorting convoys. We chatted and learned of each other's connection to the war. I told him of my brother's struggle with Post Traumatic Stress Disorder, PTSD, and he listened very intently.

"I'm one of the lucky ones," he told me. "I should have it, but I don't. I've seen a lot. One time, I saw these little kids waving at our convoy. I guess they wanted candy or something. Right about the time our Humvee got close to them, some crazy terrorist started throwing grenades at us and one of them went off right in faces of those little kids. It was really bad, but I'm okay. I shouldn't be okay, but I am. Really, if anyone should have PTSD it should be me for seeing that, right? That's why I guess I'm lucky, because I don't have it."

It was hard for me to summon a response, but my maternal instincts kicked in and I replied, "Not every soldier gets PTSD and sometimes you can get it years after you've been in combat. If you ever want to talk to someone, I've got a phone number for the counselors at the

VA. They aren't Army counselors, they are civilians. So just let me know if you ever need that number, okay?"

I handed him a piece of paper with my email address, thanked him again for serving our country, and we parted. As I drove home, my face streamed with tears while I thought about that soldier, my brother, and the thousands of others who suffer from PTSD.

PTSD is the after taste of survival. We ask our soldiers to see and do unthinkable things in combat. To survive, their minds shut down emotions and their actions become automated. It's when the mind allows those emotions to resurface that PTSD takes hold.

There are numerous videos posted online with photos and video of the Deuce Four deployment to Iraq. Most of the videos contain violent, graphic images. However, some contain photos of everyday life – Iraqi civilians and U.S. soldiers – conducting both the business of war and of existence. The soldiers that create these videos are not only sharing their experience, but also expelling some of their feelings. Sharing memories through video serves as a memorial to the comrades lost in battle and as a healing mechanism to those who returned home.

Months passed after my brother's return to the United States with Deuce Four before he was released from the Army. James' three-year contract expired while he was in Iraq. He was among the countless soldiers who had been "stop-lossed" - kept in the Army passed contract expiration. When James finally returned to our hometown after his release from the Army, I could tell that he was not the same. I told myself over and over again that time would heal his wounds.

Often, I would ask my brother if he had spoken to his friends from Deuce Four. Maybe sent an email or made a phone call. His reply was always the same. No, he was not maintaining contact and he did not seem interested in talking about the Army or the war. In fact, he didn't seem interested in much of anything.

Though I recognized serious changes in my brother immediately, I did not admit them to myself for months. He was distant at times and clingy at others. He often paused mid-sentence and would blankly stare, then return to conversation just as quickly. I suggested counseling and veterans support groups, but at the time he didn't want any part of that.

For a while, he numbed himself by drinking. A lot of drinking. It is hard to watch a young man, just 22 years-old, drink so much that he can't remember where he was or what he did. It became painfully evident that my brother had enormous problems. I knew his head injury during the war was partially to blame, but I also suspected that he was suffering from PTSD. I've come to learn that drug and alcohol abuse is common in the military.

We asked Jon about the use of alcohol by soldiers both deployed and at home.

*"While we were there, it was very dry. In country, the only way you could get alcohol was basically smuggling it. Which, I can say I'm also guilty for doing that. When I came back from leave I even smuggled a bottle. And, I had my girlfriend send me some in the mail too. Hid it inside socks and stuff like that. But, (the alcohol use) was mostly before we left for Iraq and after we got back in country. There were a lot of people that were doing a bunch of things that were, well, were very reckless. It was very common to see soldiers getting drunk every single night before we left. I was constantly called to different accidents of soldiers that had fallen or done something stupid like jump off the top of a building with a snowboard strapped to their feet. And, of course, they all had to come to me because I was one of the only medics that lived in the barracks. All the other medics were married. I'd have to say the abuse was pretty high, but, a lot like a college dorm. I mean you have all these guys that are college age, young kids. Of course they are going to drink. They have a chance to, they have disposable income, and basically no repercussions if they blew their entire check in one day. They still were gonna get fed, they still were going to have a place to live. So, they pretty much lived for the moment. As well as, a bunch of other risky things, like having unprotected sex was also a very prominent thing in the Army. Being the medic, I was exposed to a lot of that as well.*

179

*There were soldiers, before we left, that were very
scared of deploying and they were trying to get out of
the deployment. And, a lot of them went and did use
illegal drugs knowing they would get caught. Their
plan really backfired on them. They were demoted in
rank and still deployed anyway, and had some of the
worst details while we were there. But, for the most
part, the guys did not do drugs, at least not in the
barracks."*

The U.S. Army today is completely staffed by volunteers.
There is no draft, and on some level we have to
acknowledge that each of our soldiers joined having a
choice. Their choice was to adhere to the rules, regulations
and order of the military or not to join at all. While all our
soldiers may have joined voluntarily, certainly they did not
sign-up for the long-term side effects that so many of our
soldiers suffer after returning from home. From substance
abuse, to reckless conduct and emotional roller coasters,
soldiers returning from war are forced to deal with an
array of problems no regulation can direct.

After months of strange and dangerous behavior, my
brother James finally found his way to the VA Hospital.
Just as James had learned to navigate the streets of Mosul
driving the Stryker, he had to learn how to navigate the VA
system. It was challenging for him, but in a sense, it gave
him another 'mission' – something to keep him busy and
help him heal.  It was determined that the head injury my
brother suffered was far worse than originally diagnosed,
and that he was suffering from PTSD.

At least 181 Deuce Four soldiers were wounded, injured or fell ill during the fight for Mosul. Well over 300,000 soldiers from these two wars so far have reported PTSD symptoms, but only about half that number have gotten treatment.

PTSD is a mental illness. Nothing can prepare a family for the effects PTSD will have on their soldiers or their family. As with any mental illness, the entire family suffers. Were it not for Patti 'adopting' me into her family, I most certainly would not be able to deal with the effects this war has had on my own family. Looking back, I wish that in the months following my brother's return I had gotten counseling from a professional.

Today I am thankful for my brother's safe passage through the war and for the new family I now have with Patti. I am saddened, too, because although James returned in flesh, the brother I knew never came back from Iraq. His unusual behavior, bad decisions, and personality changes were extremely difficult for our family to cope with. While I mourn the loss of my brother's innocence, I know he is a survivor for which I am eternally thankful. As he told me many times during his deployment, he is tough. We have a chance at a new beginning. There are many other families far less fortunate than ours that were not been granted the opportunity for a new beginning after the war.

Every combat soldier experiences PTSD in some form, and each soldier deals with the effects differently. Learning how to manage life in spite of PTSD is the challenge for many soldiers, including my brother. I feel helplessness much the same as I felt during the deployment because there really is nothing I can do to help. The future for my brother is his own to shape. I hope he will be able to focus on a new life far away from war.

These days, my brother seems mostly hopeful and positive, making great strides to turn his life into something meaningful. Sometimes, however, he is still held by the grip of PTSD and becomes anchored by the simplest of tasks. I believe in my heart that he will recover from his injuries. In time, and with the help of the very caring and supportive staff at the VA, I trust James will be able to look more into the future than into the past and that the image he sees will be one of hope and happiness.

# FRIENDS FOR LIFE

I have many unanswered questions. Why did 3rd Platoon A-Company make it home without losing one soldier? How did Patti and I find each other in the vast sea of the internet just at the time that we needed a "combat buddy"? When will my brother and so many other soldiers recover from PTSD? Will the war in Iraq ever end?

Maybe divine intervention is responsible for bringing home every member of 3rd Platoon, including our boys. Maybe it is just about being in the right place at the right time. Maybe it is just plain being lucky, but isn't being lucky really just the same as being blessed?

Jon told us his thoughts about the survival of 3rd Platoon.

*"While we were there, no one in 3rd Platoon/A-Company was killed. Why? I really couldn't tell you why. It was very interesting to me. I felt so blessed that none of us were killed. We did have some that were injured. I remember one of the Strykers that was right behind us drove by this one car that our Stryker had driven by not 5 minutes before. That same car pulled out and hit the Stryker behind us instead, that was the Stryker with Lt Smiley. The reason behind it, I really couldn't tell anyone why. I can't understand why. It was just luck. It wasn't that we were better or better trained or anything like that. I would like to take*

*credit for that, but that really wasn't what it was about. It was just, I guess we were lucky. We had just as many close calls that could have killed us, just fractions of an inch, split seconds, things like that... we really we lucked out."*

It is so true that in this war, in any war, seconds can mean the difference between life and death. For our boys, it meant so many times that they escaped harm. For other soldiers, it meant leaving Iraq bent, but not broken. For Riikka Jacobsen and her children, seconds took a father, husband and friend from earth, but not from their hearts.

During the deployment, Patti and I spent a great deal of time sorting out the situation in Mosul and the status of our boys, day by day and even hour by hour. After they returned, we found ourselves trying to find a way to sort out the feelings and difficulties left in the wake of the war. Patti and I both have a need to put things in order. For us, writing this book has been our therapy. In a small way, it has helped us to put some order to the chaos of our lives during the deployment.

The year of deployment was filled with a plethora of emotions and unknowns. In the beginning, we used each other for information, and we used the internet to gather news and information about the boys. Ours was a united front. We could watch for each other's soldier online and relay messages for each other. Communication truly was the foundation of our friendship. Both Patti and I rely heavily on electronic communication both in the office and

184

at home. This translated into our relationships with our soldiers and each other. So many times during that year, we found ourselves turning to each other because no one else, not even our spouses, could understand how we were feeling.

I used to think online relationships were strange, until the internet brought me together with Patti. Without it, we would never have found each other – we would never have become friends for life.

---

*God must have brought us together during the deployment. There were countless hours crying, talking, pontificating and even some laughing. In the end, what we gained was a friendship that will last a lifetime.*

*I sometimes wonder….exactly what was it that made Jenn and I become such close friends. In so many ways, we are different. Jenn is young enough to easily be my daughter, had I married at an earlier age. There were a couple of other relatives of Deuce Four soldiers with whom I also communicated, but we did not become as close. Even our soldiers, Jon and James, who were in the same platoon and very close friends while in Mosul, are not close friends at the time of this writing.*

*I guess it is just that we bring out the best in each other…like the character Forrest Gump said in the now famous movie, "Me and Jenny, we're just like peas and carrots".*

185

*I could easily imagine a different scenario….after our soldiers returned and Jenn and her dad met them the day of the homecoming , and Tom and I attended the Redeployment ceremony about a month later…probably if the next event had not happened then we would have begun to drift apart.*

*In January of 2006, Rob, Jenn's husband, was scheduled to attend a college bowl game in Phoenix, Arizona, with customers. Rob casually asked Jenn if she would like to accompany him and take a day to visit with her "friend" in Arizona. I actually just learned this, and as I look back, I am amazed how Rob sensed our closeness even that long ago, with little direct knowledge about who Tom and I were, and he was happy to have our friendship grow even stronger. Jenn called and asked if Tom and I would be home for a visit, and just like that, we had our first visit planned. Jenn and I knew each other over the phone and via Instant Message, but this would be our first face-to-face meeting. Tom knew Jenn from similar but fewer IM and telephone contacts. Tom and I knew of Rob only through Jenn. For all of us, there was little doubt that we would instantly bond and grow in love and respect for each other.*

*Surely, you can guess from the title of this book that our visit that January was very enjoyable. We learned more about each other's lives, and found many of our philosophies were the same. We talked with Rob and Jenn about our summer cottage in Canada, and invited them to join us there in the summer. We parted, looking forward to our next opportunity to get together.*

*Of course we were delighted when summer came and Jenn, Grant, and Dixie, their dog, drove from Indiana north to our* cottage for a week of fun in the sun, water, and pure air of our beloved Sandy Island. The stories they took home sold Rob on joining the trip in the summers to follow. Since that time, every summer we vacation together for a week in Canada. They are now part of our family and we all count the days through the winter until we will be together again on Sandy Island.

Jenn is like the daughter I never had. She is a spark of energy and optimism. She teaches me all the time about "new things" and encourages me in so many ways. We are what my 84-year-old father would call a" Mutual Admiration Society".

Many men form friendships for life during deployments while serving together on the battlefield. But when you think about war, you rarely think about the families back home that become friends for life. It is certain that the two of us would never otherwise have met and become friends. Now, we could not dream of a greater blessing to have emerged from our year of deployment We are sisters not in blood, but by choice, in this walk of life. We are here for each other, no matter the next trials that may come.

# APPENDIXES

## TIMELINE

**September 11, 2001:** Terrorists attack the United States
**June 2003:** Deuce Four travels to Ft. Knox, KY, with their
Stryker vehicles to participate in the Initial Operational Test
and Evaluation (IOT&E) of the vehicles, readying for combat
**August 2003:** Deuce Four travels to South Korea to
demonstrate the Stryker vehicle capabilities
**October 20, 2004:** Deuce Four replaces the 3rd Brigade in
Mosul as terrorist uprising escalates.
**November 2004:** As U.S. Forces push hard against the
insurgency in Fallujah, terrorists flee in hordes to Mosul,
creating a perilous situation for Deuce Four
**December 21, 2004:** A suicide bomber detonates a bomb
inside the mess hall at FOB Marez, Mosul, Iraq
**January 30, 2005:** Iraqi people across the country participate
in first general election held since the U.S. invasion in 2003.
Despite fierce attacks from insurgents in Mosul, Deuce Four
is able to provide safe polling sites for thousands of voters.
**March 31, 2005:** Washington Post publishes an article about
the Stryker vehicle, questioning the vehicles safety and
readiness for combat.
**September 17, 2005:** Homecoming at Ft. Lewis
**October 27, 2005:** Redeployment Ceremony
**September 2008:** Jenn and Patti begin writing Friend for Life

## CARE PACKAGES

Sending care packages is an easy way to support troops. No matter where in the world your soldier is stationed, by simply using the APO address assigned to them, you will pay the same postage rates as if you were shipping the package to an address in the United States. Packages with lots of heavy items, such as canned foods, can be quite heavy. Luckily, the US Postal Service offers flat rate Priority Mail. Anything you can fit into a flat rate box costs just one low price. This service was introduced while our boys were in Iraq and it was such fantastic news! Not only did we take advantage of flat rate shipping, but we also discovered that the USPS provides FREE boxes, tape and labels for Priority Mail! Simply logon to www.USPS.com and order the supplies needed.

## Ideas to make your care package special!

1.Homemade cookies, brownies, and rice cereal treats can all be packed with a food sealer, or wrapped in plastic wrap and storage bags

2.Entertainment – DVDs, CDs and MP3 players

3.Theme boxes

•birthday party in a box (balloons, party favors, prepacked cupcakes, and a disposable camera to preserve the memory

•water balloon party in a box

4.Insect repellent, battery or DC powered personal sized fans, hand warming packs (for the winter months)

5.Coffee, flavored creamer, flavor packets for water bottles, assorted teas

6.Books, magazines and clippings – rather than sending the entire newspaper, clip articles from home that will appeal to your soldier (only one bible per soldiers is allowed, so ask before shipping)

7.Snacks – beef jerky, nuts, candy (send chocolate only Oct -- Feb), Ramen noodles, crackers, peanut butter, jelly, foil packed tuna, canned pasta (remember to pack a can opener if you send canned goods), soup (avoid pull tab cans as they can open during transit if handled roughly), trail mix, instant oatmeal packets, condiment packets (ketchup, mustard, hot sauce, mayo, vinegar), powdered drink mixes such as Gatorade

8.Toiletries – the military provides toiletries, but soldiers often miss their favorite items from home. Send full size when possible. Foot powder and sunscreen suggested.

9.Headlamp (flashlight with head strap)

10.Games – any type of video game, board games, playing cards, Frisbee, Nerf balls and toys (don't forget batteries)

# SUPPORT FOR OUR SOLDIERS

## EMOTIONAL AND PHYSICAL SUPPORT

**The Soldiers Project**
Provides free, unlimited, confidential mental health services to service members and their extended families who have served in Iraq and Afghanistan.
877.576.5343, toll free or 818.761.7438, direct in California
info@thesoldiersproject.org

**Operation Homefront**
Provides emergency and morale assistance for our troops, the families they leave behind and for the wounded warriors when they return home. Operation Homefront is a national nonprofit.
Contact Amy Palmer, Chief Operating Officer
8930 Fourwinds DR STE 340, San Antonio, TX 78239
800.722.6098, toll free
www.operationhomefront.net
www.homefrontonline.com

**National Center for Post Traumatic Stress Disorder**
Promotes issues related to PTSD and maintains an extensive website - www.ncptsd.va.gov

**USA National Suicide Hotlines**
If you are in emotional distress, suicidal, or concerned about someone who might be, this lifeline is available to help. Operates toll-free, 24 hours a day, 7 days a week. 800.SUICIDE (1.800.784.2433), toll free
800.273.TALK (1.800.273.8255), alternate toll free number
800.799.4TTY (4889), TTY
www.suicidehotlines.com

**Community of Veterans**
A joint effort of the Iraq and Afghanistan Veterans of America (IAVA) and the Ad Council, Their website is designed as a resource to our nation's newest Veterans. While addressing a range of topics, this site is ultimately a point of connection where Veterans are helping Veterans. IAVA was founded in 2004, and is the nation's first and largest group representing veterans of the wars in Iraq and Afghanistan. IAVA is a non-profit and nonpartisan organization.
Write IAVA, 770 Broadway, 2nd FL, New York, NY 10003
www.communityofveterans.org

## HELP FOR THE WOUNDED
**Angels of Mercy Program**
Supports our wounded military and their families.
Contact Jay Edwards and Marian Chirichella, Founders
703.938.8930, direct phone
Write in c/o American Legion Auxiliary Unit 270, PO Box 3310, McLean, VA 22101
oifoefangels@aol.com
www.SupportOurWounded.org

**Comfort for America's Uniformed Services (C.A.U.S.E.)**
Organizes recreation and entertainment programs for wounded warriors recuperating at military medical facilities from injuries received in Iraq and Afghanistan.
Contact Barbara Lau, Executive Director
703.750.6458, direct phone
Write 6315 Bren Mar DR, STE 175, Alexandria, VA 22312
info@cause-usa.org
www.cause-usa.org

**The American Soldier Foundation**
Assists soldiers on extended active duty and their dependents, and the dependents of those lost in the line of duty. The Foundation can provide grants or interest-free loans for food, rent, utilities, funeral expenses, counseling, medical expenses, and other basic needs.
Write 18 Wood PL, Manhasset, NY 11030
contact@soldierfoundation.org
www.soldierfoundation.org

**Fisher House Foundation, Inc.**
Fisher Houses are located on the grounds of all of the major military medical centers and many VA medical centers, providing a "home away from home" for families of patients receiving medical care.
Write 111 Rockville Pike, ST 420, Rockville, MD 20850
888.294.8560, toll free
www.fisherhouse.org

**Intrepid Fallen Heroes Fund**
Has provided more than $65 million in support for the families of military personnel lost in service to our nation and for severely wounded military personnel and veterans through projects like the Center for the Intrepid at Brooke Army Medical Center in San Antonio, TX specializing in amputee and severe burn patients and the new National Intrepid Center of Excellence for traumatic brain injury and psychological health at the National Naval Medical Center in Bethesda, Maryland.
Write 1 Intrepid SQ, W 46th ST & 12th AVE, New York , NY 10036
800.340.HERO, toll free
info@fallenheroesfund.org
www.fallenheroesfund.org

## HOUSING NEEDS

### Military Housing Assistance Fund

MHAF works to help military families realize the American dream they are defending by providing a grant to help pay the closing costs associated with the purchase of their home and this grant is a free gift that they never have to repay.
720.932.8049, direct phone
Write 1400 16th ST, STE 400, Denver, CO 80202
www.militaryhousingassistancefund.com

## VETERAN EMPLOYMENT SUPPORT

### Hire America's Heroes

Engages corporations in activities designed to educate, promote, and facilitate recognized best-practice processes and success strategies for sourcing, recruiting, hiring, on-boarding, supporting, and retaining America's military service members and veterans. Individual service members may access information regarding job opportunities, a network to help service members find great civilian careers, and enhanced corporate understanding of the value veterans bring to the corporate workplace.
425.301.5445, direct phone
Write PO Box 407, Redmond, WA 98073
info@hireamericasheroes.org
www.hireamericasheroes.org

## FAMILY SUPPORT

### Clint Gertson Memorial/Scholarship Freedom Fund

Honor the memory of Clint Gertson with a donation to the Clint Gertson Memorial. Mail donations to Gertson Memorial Scholarship Fund, c/o First National Bank of Eagle Lake, PO Box 247, Eagle Lake, TX 77434

## The Armed Forces Foundation

Provides a wide variety of assistance, including financial, educational, and social services.

202.547.4713, direct phone

Write Armed Forces Foundation, 16 North Carolina AVE, SE Washington, DC 20003

www.armedforcesfoundation.org

## American Military Family

Honors and supports all members of the United States Military and their families, who together serve and sacrifice so much for all of us as they protect and defend our freedom. Request aid, apply for a grant, or make a donation to AMF Programs.

Contact Debbie Quackenbush, Founder

303.746.8195, direct phone

Write PO Box 625, Niwot, CO 80544

www.amf100.org

## Children of Fallen Soldiers Relief Fund, Inc.

Provides financial assistance to surviving and severely disabled service members' children affected by OEF or OIF as well as college scholarships to the surviving spouses, children and disabled service members and their children.

Write PO Box 3968, Gaithersburg, MD 20885

866. 96.CFSRF, toll free

301. 685.3421, direct

www.childrenoffallensoldiersrelieffund.org

## Association of the United States Army

AUSA is a private, non-profit educational organization that supports America's Army including Active Duty, National Guard, Reserves, Civilians, Retirees and family members. Through our more than 120 chapters worldwide, AUSA offers a variety of services and programs in support of soldiers and their families.

800.335.4570, toll free
Write 2425 Wilson Blvd., Arlington, VA 22201
www.ausa.org (select 'chapter activities' on the home page, then select your state for chapter locations and contacts)

## LETTERS, MESSAGES & CARE PACKAGES
### Adopt-a-Platoon Soldier Support Effort
A nonprofit organization dedicated to United States deployed Service Members to provide a better deployment quality of life, lift morale, and assist military families.
Contact Ida Hägg
956.748.4145, direct phone
Write PO Box 234, Lozano, TX 78568
info@adoptaplatoon.org
www.adoptaplatoon.org

### Any Soldier Inc.
Send your support to a Soldier in harm's way.
Contact Marty Horn, SFC, USA MP, Retired and President of Any Soldier Inc.
Write PO Box 29, Hoagland, IN 46745
www.AnySoldier.com

### Operation Care Packages
Works to ensure no hero is forgotten through care packages, supplies, phone cards and letters of support to our deployed and wounded soldiers, and Veterans.
Contact Debbie Smothers
815.693.3215, direct
Write 611 Wilcox ST, Joliet, IL 60435
proudarmysis4@sbcglobal.net
www.operationcarepackages.org

## Operation Gratitude

A California-based non-profit, volunteer organization that sends care packages of snacks, entertainment items and personal letters of appreciation addressed to individually named U.S. Service Members deployed in hostile regions such as Iraq and Afghanistan, and on military ships at sea. Contact Carolyn Blashek, Founder

818.909.0039, direct phone

Write 16444 Refugio RR, Encino, CA 91436 opgrat@gmail.com

www.operationgratitude.com

## Operation Military Support

Send packages overseas weekly to including personal hygiene items, snacks, and entertainment.

209.763.2766, direct phone

Write PO Box 901, San Andreas, CA 95249

oms@operationmilitarysupport.com

www.OperationMilitarySupport.com

## Packages from Home

Sends care and comfort packages to deployed American military heroes who are stationed in active duty theaters around the world, as well as to facilitate activities that elevate morale of all veterans.

Contact Ms. Kathleen Lewis, Founder

602.254.2818, direct phone

Write 1201 S 7th AVE, STE 50, Phoenix, AZ 85007

info@packagesfromhome.org www.PackagesFromHome.org

## The Kitchen Table Gang Trust

Veterans helping other veterans and our troops overseas.

Contact Charles Taliaferro, Director

Write 42922 Avenue 12, Madera, CA, 93636

www.kitchentablegang.org

**Operation We Care**
Sends care packages to the troops deployed to Iraq and Afghanistan. Monthly packages include personal items, snacks and letters.
Contact Brenda Ogden, President
985.892.9700, direct phone
Write 67029 Locke ST, Mandeville, LA 70471
www.operationwecare.com

**A Million Thanks**
Provides U.S. military men and women stationed at home and abroad with thank you letters to encourage their efforts.
Contact Shauna Fleming
714.925.1211, direct phone
17583 Santiago BLVD, 107-355, Villa Park, CA 92861
www.amillionthanks.org

**Give2TheTroops, Inc.®**
Supports America's armed forces in combat zones around the world through the letters and packages prepared and shipped by caring volunteers.™ A non-profit organization, donations to are tax deductible.
Contact Andi Grant, President and Founder
888.876.6775, toll free
Write 196 West ST, Rocky Hill, CT 06067
Andi@Give2thetroops.org
www.give2thetroops.org

**Marine Parents, Inc.**
Provides support, information and services for Marines and their families, and encourages troop support through community awareness programs.
573.303.5500, direct phone (press 411 for a complete directory of services, support and outreach programs)

Write PO Box 1115, Columbia, MO 65205
www.marineparents.com

**Soldiers Angels**
Soldiers Angels provides aid and comfort to members of the military and their families.
Contact Ms. Patti Patton-Bader, President and Founder
626.529.5114, direct
Write 1792 E. Washington Blvd, Pasadena, CA 91104
pbader@soldiersangers.org
www.soldiersangels.org

## PHONE CARDS
### Cell Phones for Soldiers
Cell Phones for Soldiers, Inc. raises funds through the recycling of used cell phones collected at drop off sites throughout the USA, Cell Phones for Soldiers, Inc. to provide free prepaid calling cards to troops deployed around the world.
Contact Brittany and Robbie Bergquist
cellphonesforsoldiers@yahoo.com
www.cellphonesforsoldiers.com

## ENTERTAINMENT FOR THE TROOPS
### Stars for Stripes, Inc.
A non-profit organization dedicated to providing quality celebrity entertainment to internationally deployed U.S. military forces.
Contact Judy Seale
615.872.2122, direct
Write 109 Rivers Edge Ct, Nashville, Tennessee, 37214
Judy@starsforstripes.com
www.starsforstripes.com

## DEPLOYMENT SURVIVAL TIPS

•Do not expect friends, co-workers or even some family members to understand how you feel.

•Display your support with bumper stickers, a blue star banner, shirts, pins and flags.

•Expect to feel a wide array of emotions, including anger, grief and depression.

•Constantly watching the news won't do you or your soldier any good. Take breaks from the television and internet..

•Beware of the temptations of alcohol and drugs. Your soldier needs you to stay healthy and strong.

•Do not ask your soldier to share information about their missions or location.

•Keep a journal and copies of your emails and IMs. You'll find it to be therapeutic both during the deployment and after when you have time to reflect and heal.

•Write letters and send care packages. This is as beneficial to you as it is to your soldier.

•Connect with other families of the deployed soldiers.

•If you feel desperate, severely depressed, or suicidal, seek professional help. USA National Suicide Hotlines operate toll-free, 24 hours a day, 7 days a week.

Tel. 1.800.SUICIDE (1.800.784.2433)
Toll Free 1.800.273.TALK (1.800.273.8255)
TTY: 1.800.799.4TTY (4889)

# LETTERS FROM BASIC TRAINING

Basic Training at Ft. Benning lasts 14 weeks. That's a very long time for any young man who has never really been away from home. It is also a long time for an overprotective older sister/legal guardian/parent. A week or two into basic training, drill instructors order the recruits to write home.

Letter from James Smith, spring 2002, from Ft. Benning.

**Dear Jenn,**

**Well, I made it to basic and I'm doing fine. We are getting into good shape here, doing lots of push ups and exercises and marches every day. The food is great and I am eating a ton and I have made a couple of friends. There are people here from all over the place. I'm learning a lot and doing a bunch of stuff that I never thought I would be doing.**

**I hope you can come to the turning blue ceremony. It would be great to see you guys. Write me if you can come. Pet Dixie for me and tell Grant and Dad and Rob I said hi. Don't worry about me. It's not as hard here as I thought. It's not that bad at all, really. You have my address now, so write me if you can. Can you give Dad my address, too? Love you guys.**

**Your Brother,**

**James**

Letter from Jon Donahue, summer 2003, from Ft. Sill.

*Hey Guys,*

*Just thought that I would write again. Got a free moment and thought I would scribble down some things about basic training.*

*Every day at 0400, we wake up and do 50 – 100 pushups and 50 – 100 Butterfly kicks. Then we clean up the bunks and our wall lockers. Then we scrub and polish the showers and toilets until 0450 witch seems like a long time but believe me we haven't made many days without doing pushups for screwing up. We all are really tired from the time change. No one (except the drill sergeants) is used to the time changes.*

*After cleaning we go to the field and stretch out for running. My legs are really sore from the running and the marching. The worst thing is the waiting. You have been on your feet marching everywhere and then you suddenly stop and stand somewhere for ten to twenty minutes. Your legs start burning but you can't move cause you are at attention. The boots I got are starting to break in and the inserts that I got help a little. The only problem I have is that the shoe size I have is a 14 wide and the biggest insoles are 13 narrow. That is at the PX though and I messed up ...bought only one pair, so I have one pair of comfortable boots and one not so good pair. I have noticed that my feet smell a lot better then the rest of the platoon's feet because of the foot powder.*

*After the running we go to chow. The really neat thing about going to the mess hall is we get to see and talk to the more advanced platoons that are in week 8 or above (even though we aren't suppose to talk in mess hall). It is neat to hear about the 15k marches and the tenting experience. Each private is given a half a tent so each private must depend on their battle buddy for shelter. We are expecting a 2K march with LBE. An LBE is two canteens and a belt with a small arms cases. They are neat but very old. Most of the straps are broken or torn up.*

*After mess hall breakfast we march to either the barracks to clean or to a class room to learn. Most of the training has been about how to keep clean, and to make sure that we have enough water in our system. Then we march to chow again and eat. After that we have been learning facing movements. It is really neat with the games we play. One is called Knock Out. The point of the game is to listen closely to the drill sergeant. He tried to trick you by giving the wrong command. I normally make it to the top ten and once I won the game and did a moon walk in celebration. After that we change out of our BDUs into our PTUs and shine our boots. Then we eat and then shower unless we pissed off the drill sergeant. Then we do more Physical Training...on the grass on the slope of a hill! It is really hard to do a push up on a steep hill. Then we* *go to sleep. At the end of the day you are really ready to put your head down for the day. I failed my first PT test, but most people in all the platoons did. Before we all did our sit-ups the master sergeant made us all do Butterfly Kicks and pushups while we were waiting because of two or three people that need a boot in their a\*\* to get them to shut up. I had to wait ten minutes for my turn and then  it was hard to do the first sit up. I don't feel too bad though because only nine people passed. I did well on the other test, 49 pushups and a 15:47 mile run.*

*I found out that I can have pictures, but No Nude ones. So tell my brothers to keep their clothes on! I miss you all very much. I can't wait to see you soon.*

*Love, Jonathan*

# GLOSSARY

**AD** - Active Duty
**AG** - Adjutant General
**AIT** - Advanced Individual Training
**AMMO** - Ammunition
**APO** - Army Post Office
**AR** - Army Reserve or Army Regulation or Armor
**ASAP** - As Soon As Possible
**ASVAB** - Armed Services Vocational Aptitude Battery
**AWOL** - Absent Without Leave
**BCT** - Basic Combat Training
**BDE** - Brigade
**BDU** - Battle Dress Uniform or "cammos"
**BN** - Battalion
**CDR** - Commander
**CG** - Commanding General
**CLASS A's** - Dress Uniform: dark green suit, green shirt, tie
**CLASS B's** - Class A's with the suit jacket left off
**CNO** – Casualty Notification Officer
**CO** - Commanding Officer/Company
**COB** - Close of Business
**COL** - Colonel
**COLA** - Cost of Living Allowance
**CP** - Command Post
**CPL** - Corporal
**CPT** - Captain
**CSM** – Command Sergeant Major
**DA** - Department of the Army
**DI** - Drill Instructor
**DO** - Duty Officer
**DOB** - Date of Birth
**DOD** - Department of Defense

**DS** - Drill Sergeant
**EE** - Emergency Essential
**EEO** - Equal Employment Opportunity
**EN** - Enlisted
**ETS** - Estimated Time of Separation
**FDU** - Full Dress Uniform
**FLO** - Family Liaison Office
**FOB** - Forward Operations Base or Forward Operating Base
**FOUO** - For Official Use Only
**FRG** – Family Readiness Group
**FRO** - Family Readiness Officer
**FSG** - Family Support Group
**FTX** - Field Training Exercise
**GED** - General Education Diploma
**GEN** -  General
**GI** - Government Issue
**HAJJI**– American soldier slang for Iraqi people
**HEAD**- restroom
**HHC** - Headquarters and Headquarters Company
**HOOAH** - slang for "okay"or "I understand"
**HOR** - Home of Record
**HQ** - Headquarters
**HS** - Home station
**IM** – Instant Message
**ING** - Iraqi National Guard
**IO** - Information Officer
**IRF** - Immediate Reaction Force
**JAG** - Judge Advocate General
**JOE** - slang for an enlisted soldier under your  command
**KIA** - Killed In Action
**LOD** - Line of Duty
**LT** - Lieutenant ( such as 1LT or 1$^{st}$ Lieutenant)
**LTC** -  Lietenant Colonel
**MAJ** -  Major

**MEPS** - Military Enlistment Processing Center, the first stage of entry into military service

**MFO** - Multinational Forces and Observer

**MI** - Military Intelligence

**MIA** - Missing In Action

**MOS** - Military Occupational Specialty or job assigned to soldier

**MP** - Military Police

**MRE** - Meals Ready to Eat

**MSG** - Master Sergeant

**MSO** - Morale Support Officer

**NCO** - Noncommissioned Officer

**NCOIC** - Noncommissioned Officer In Charge

**NLT** - Not Later Than

**OIC** - Officer-in-Charge

**OJT** - On the Job Training

**ORE** - Operational Readiness Exercise

**OUTSIDE THE WIRE** - slang meaning operations outside base

**PAO** - Public Affairs Officer

**PDQ** - Pretty Damn Quick

**PFC** - Private First Class

**PLT** - Platoon

**POA** - Power of Attorney

**POC** - Point of Contact

**POGS** – People/Personnel Other than Grunts (non-combat soldiers/civilians on base)

**POV** - Privately Owned Vehicle

**PT** - Physical Training

**PVT or PV2** - Private

**PX** - Post Exchange, place to purchase groceries and supplies

**QTRS** - Quarters (living area)

**RA** - Regular Army

**RD** - Rear Detachment, aka Rear D

**RDC** - Rear Detachment Commander

**RDF** - Rapid Deployment Force

**R&D** - Research and Development
**REG** - Regulation
**REGT** - Regiment
**R&R** - Rest and Recreation
**RIF** - Reduction in Force
**ROTC** - Reserve Officer Training Corps
**SFC** - Sergeant First Class
**SGM** - Sergeant Major
**SGT** - Sergeant
**SOP** - Standing Operating Procedure
**SQD**- Squad, a unit within a platoon
**SPC** - Specialist
**SRB** - Selective Reenlistment Bonus
**SSG** - Staff Sergeant
**SSN** - Social Security Number
**STOP-LOSS** - involuntary military contract extension
**STRYKER** - 8-Wheel Armored Combat Vehicle
**TAG** - The Adjutant General
**TASC** - Training and Support Center
**TBI** - Traumatic Brain Injury
**TDY** - Temporary Duty
**TIG** - Time in Grade
**TTYL** – Instant Message abbreviation for 'talk to you later'
**USPS** – United States Postal Service
**VA** - Department of Veterans Affairs
**VAMC** - Veterans Affairs Medical Center
**VHA** - Veterans Health Administration
**XO** - Executive Officer

# ABOUT THE AUTHORS

**IN TELLING, YOU CAN FIND MEANING.**

Jennifer MackInday lives in Bloomington, Indiana, with her husband, Rob, and son, Grant. She attended Indiana University and has spent much of her career in advertising and marketing. Jennifer is a freelance writer and the owner of several successful enterprises, the latest of which is Sandy Island Press, publishing company for <u>Friends for Life</u>. Jennifer believes her faith in God guides and comforts her through all things. She enjoys gardening, reading, and cooking. Author of several pieces for magazines and periodicals, this is Jennifer's first book.

*Patti Donahue splits her time between Amado, Arizona, and Sandy Island in Ontario, Canada. She has been married for over 30 years to Tom, and has three grown sons, Tommy, Jon and Chris, to whom she credits her inspiration, along with love of her Savior Jesus and the desire to share the free gift of salvation. Early in her career, when asked to list her priorities, Patti quickly stated, "God, Family, Career." With that philosophy as her guiding principle, Patti has successfully balanced her family life and career as a corporate Director. Having worked more than 16 years in Mexico, she often describes herself as a true NAFTA woman.* <u>Friends For Life</u> *is her first published work.*